500

green and detox juices

500

green and detox juices

the only compendium of green & detox drinks you'll ever need

Carol Beckerman

SELLERS
PUBLISHING

A Quintet Book

Published by Sellers Publishing, Inc.
161 John Roberts Road, South Portland, Maine 04106
Visit our Web site: www.sellerspublishing.com
E-mail: rsp@rsvp.com

ISBN: 978-1-4162-4562-9
Library of Congress Control Number: 2015930716
QTT.FHGR

This book was conceived, designed and produced by
Quintet Publishing Limited
4th Floor, Sheridan House
114-116 Western Road
Hove, East Sussex
BN3 1DD

Food Stylist: Carol Beckerman
Photographer: Jon Whitaker
Editor: Salima Hirani
Designer: Rod Teasdale
Art Director: Michael Charles
Editorial Assistant: Ella Lines
Editorial Director: Emma Bastow
Publisher: Mark Searle

Quintet would like to thank Andrew James UK Ltd www.andrewjamesworldwide.
com and Phillips https://www.philips.co.uk for the juicers and blenders used in the
photography.

Disclaimer: The information in this book is not intended as medical advice, diagnosis,
or prescription. You should always consult a doctor or other health-care professional.
10 9 8 7 6 5 4 3 2 1

Printed in China by 1010 Printing International Ltd.

contents

introduction

"Don't injure your system by over-feeding it. Over-eating will kill you long before your time." **Paul Bragg**

Have you eaten too many doughnuts? Have the holidays taken a toll on your digestion? Do you want to detox and kick-start a healthy eating plan?

If the answer to all those questions is "yes", there is a one-word solution – "juicing."

In the Western world we are in the middle of an over-eating epidemic. Juice cleanses are all around us, and there is a good reason for that. Effective at boosting your health, and a great substitute for a sugar-loaded snack, juices can have a fast and positive impact on your vitality and mood. It has often been said that food is medicine, and when you are benefiting from a glass of fresh and vibrant vegetable and fruit juice, that can certainly be the case.

A healthy lifestyle is one of the keys to longevity, and there are myriad health benefits that come from drinking freshly prepared juice. As the produce retains most of the vitamins, minerals, enzymes, and plant chemicals that are usually killed off by the heat in the cooking process, it is a great way to add nutrients to your diet that you normally wouldn't eat. As the juicer does most of the digesting for you, the nutrients are turbocharged straight into your system, and can help protect against cardiovascular problems and inflammatory diseases such as rheumatoid arthritis. There are valuable compounds in fresh juices that can guard against cellular damage, which is made worse by exposure to chemicals and pollution. Juicing is not a substitute for eating the whole fruit or vegetable, as you lose the added benefits of their complex fibers, but it is a great way to get a burst of nutrition, and an excellent way to meet your five-a-day quota. Children especially will enjoy the bright colors

and fresh tastes of juices made from their favorite fruits. They will never know about the hidden vegetables, and so get a nourishing after-school snack without lots of sugar or salt.

If you suffer from food intolerances, it can be very difficult to pinpoint the particular foods that cause you problems. A juice plan lasting for up to one week is a really good elimination diet, omitting all the usual culprits that cause allergic reactions, such as dairy, wheat, and yeast. It will also stop food cravings and chocolate addictions, and will work miracles on a bloated tummy.

why juicing is so good for you

- Juicing gives you a fast delivery of nutrition

- Juicing helps you to absorb all the nutrients from vegetables

- Drinking juices allows you to consume a wide variety of fruits and vegetables in an efficient manner

- Using juices, you can easily follow an elimination diet to help you pinpoint allergies.

Juicing is not a magic weight-loss bullet. It is a quick way of loading up on disease-battling, anti-aging antioxidants, minerals, and vitamins, and can actually cause weight gain if you are not careful. Liquid calories do not register fullness like solid calories, so you may consume more calories overall if you just add juice to your diet. So you should have juice instead of a snack, or take juice as a breakfast or lunch on the go.

If you decide to pursue a diet that predominantly consists of juice, such as a detox or cleanse diet, do not do it for more than five to seven days at the most. Ensure that you consume about 2,000 calories every day, and do not starve yourself. It is important that your body gets sufficient calories, vitamins, nutrients, protein, fat, and carbohydrates. Also, make sure that you add dissolvable fiber powder to your juices, to keep your digestive system working smoothly, or instead, add plenty of fiber-rich foods, such as prunes and pears.

Whether it is to improve your health, boost your immunity, or to just feel really good, juice drinkers swear by their juicy concoctions.

techniques

A question often asked is whether to blend or to juice. As a general rule, if the fruit or vegetable is soft, such as a banana or mango, it can be peeled and blended. If it is dense or tough, such as a carrot or zucchini, it does not need to be peeled and it can be juiced. The juice can then be served straight from the juicer, or it can be transferred to a blender and other ingredients such as ice or superfood powders can be added before it is blended and served. Instructions are included in the recipes for when to peel, or remove skin, pits, and seeds.

Always scrub vegetables and fruit well with a hard brush under cold water before adding to the juicer, as germs, pesticides, and bacteria can be present on the outside. If there is a waxy residue, use a little mild soap detergent to dissolve it before rinsing under cold water.

Most juicers can be washed very easily. Rinse the removable parts under hot running water after each use, and scrub any blades or graters carefully to remove residue.

Some people sometimes like to use the pulp that is left behind to put into muffins, especially if it is quite moist, and mostly from sweeter vegetables and fruit. Otherwise, dispose of it in the rubbish bin or add it to compost. Dry all the parts of the juicer, or leave them to drain completely, before reassembling the machine.

juicers and other juicing equipment

There is no getting away from it — if you are serious about long-term juicing for health, you will need a juicer. Two types of product are popular: centrifugal and masticating. A centrifugal juicer chops up fruits and vegetables with a flat cutting blade and simultaneously spins them at a very high speed to separate the juice from the pulp. A masticating juicer works more slowly, as the fruits and vegetables are crushed and squeezed to drain the juice, while the pulp is squeezed out at the end of a tube. Masticating juicers process leafy greens and wheatgrass better than centrifugal juicers, and the juice tends to last longer. Juice from a centrifugal juicer should be consumed immediately, as nutrients will quickly be lost. Centrifugal juicers work more quickly than masticating juicers and are usually less expensive.

You will also need a good-quality blender, preferably one that is high powered enough to crush ice. This means that you can blend the juices together with other ingredients, such as milk, coconut water, or coconut milk, and make them into smoothies, which look like milkshakes and are very attractive to children. When adding larger fruit to the blender, chop it into smaller pieces. Also, remove the skin, pits, and seeds from soft fruits before blending them. Add all the ingredients to the blender at the same time – if you try to blend the fruit without adding additional liquid, the blades will not work effectively.

The magic bullet is another form of blender. It is a very high-speed blender that is ideal for a single serving of juice. You can put chopped raw vegetables and cabbage leaves into the container and the machine will crush and blend them, and all the pulp is incorporated. Consuming the pulp gives you the benefit of the fiber from the vegetables and fruit, too. Because the resulting juice can be quite dense, usually a little liquid is added with the produce during the blending process.

Always read the instruction manual from the manufacturer of your product before using your equipment for the first time.

ingredients

When juicing, try to buy fruits and vegetables that have been organically grown to avoid taking in pesticides and herbicides with your juice. For maximum freshness and flavor, prepare the fruit and vegetables just before you want to use them.

If you are overweight, have high blood pressure, diabetes, or high cholesterol, choose juice recipes that limit the number of fruits until you normalize these conditions. The exceptions to this are lemons and limes, which have virtually none of the offending sugar or fructose that causes metabolic complications. And they are amazing at eliminating the bitter taste of the dark green leafy vegetables that provide most of the benefits of juicing.

It is important to note that vegetable juice contains very little protein and almost no fat, so is not a complete food on its own. You can add protein powder and other nutritionally superior powders such as green superfood, lucuma, and maca to your juices, which will increase the nutritional impact on your system.

All the recipes in this book make one serving. This is because the juice you make should be consumed immediately, rather than made in a large quantity and some of it saved for later. If you find that the juice is too thick for your personal preference, you can thin it with water, coconut water, or any type of milk or yogurt. Mix the liquid into the juice in the blender, or simply stir it into the finished juice.

When using yogurt, try the full-fat version to keep the sugar content low, because in low-fat yogurt, the fat is replaced with sugar. Pineapple should have the outer skin removed before juicing. Almond or rice milk should preferably be unsweetened, but if preferred, you can use sweetened. When blending grapes, berries, and currants, remove the stalks and leaves and wash the fruit thoroughly. An easy way to remove the berries from the stalks of black currants or red currants is to hold the bunch firmly at the top and slowly draw the tines of a fork through the fruit so that the currants fall away. When choosing celery, bear in mind that, for the purposes of the recipes in this book, a stalk of celery should be roughly 10-in (25-cm) long.

To blend fruit in a food processor, put the chopped fruit into the bowl and process to a thick pulp. Add liquid, such as milk, coconut water, fruit juice, or yogurt, and process again.

If using an immersion blender, remember that it is not as powerful as a blender or food processor, so is only suitable for use with very soft fruits, such as bananas, ripe peaches, and berries.

More and more people are discovering the health-giving benefits of superfoods such as goji berries and acai berries. A superfood is a food that offers superior nutritional value for the amount of calories that it contains. In the recipes throughout this book, you will find additions such as green superfood powder, maca powder, and lucuma powder, all of which are considered superfoods due to their incredible antioxidant properties.

breakfast juices

In this chapter you will find recipes for juice mixes that are ideal for breakfast time, such as those with added oats, nuts, or protein powder. These power-packed juices will wake you up and get you out and about in no time—and they will keep you full and energetic until lunchtime.

blueberry & cherry

see variations page 37

Cherries are an amazing fruit with myriad health benefits. For instance, they help to reduce inflammation to ease the symptoms for sufferers of gout and arthritis, and have natural painkilling properties. Cherry anthocyanins (pigments) have been shown to protect blood vessels and brain cells against oxidative stress, suggesting that cherry consumption may help to prevent neurodegenerative diseases such as dementia. It has been claimed that cherry anthocyanins also slow the growth of human colon cancer cells. And if that isn't enough to encourage you to eat them, they are delicious, too!

1 cup blueberries
3/4 cup pitted cherries
1 cup pure acai juice

1/2 cup plain or vanilla yogurt
1 tbsp. quick-cooking rolled oats
1/2 tsp. vanilla extract

Place all the ingredients in a blender with a handful of ice. Blend until smooth.

breakfast berries

see variations page 38

All fruits and vegetables contain antioxidants (which can help to fight the oxidative stress caused by free radicals, that can lead to illness), but nutrient-rich berries are some of the best sources of antioxidants. They contain vitamin C, which boosts collagen, and this helps to maintain cartilage stores and aid in joint flexibility.

1 fuji or gala apple
1/4 small pineapple
1/2 cup raspberries
3/4 cup hulled strawberries
1/2 cup whole milk

1 tbsp. ground flaxseed
1 tbsp. quick-cooking rolled oats
1/2 tsp. ground ginger
1/2 tsp. ground cinnamon

Juice the apple and pineapple, then transfer the juice to a blender. Add the remaining ingredients and a handful of ice. Blend until smooth.

spicy grapefruit & strawberry juice with mint

see variations page 39

This is a great immune-boosting morning juice. Use sweet pink grapefruit and ripe strawberries for a delicious, refreshing drink. The rich pink color of grapefruit is due to lycopene, a nutrient found only in pink and red grapefruit (not white grapefruit). Lycopene appears to have anti-tumor properties, as well as a high capacity to help fight compounds that can damage cells. One word of warning, though — grapefruit can react with some medication, so if you are on any regular medication, check the details to ensure you can safely consume this fruit.

1 pink grapefruit, peeled
1/4 medium pineapple
1/2-in. (1-cm) piece fresh gingerroot
5 mint leaves

1 3/4 cups hulled strawberries
2 tsp. quick-cooking rolled oats
2 tsp. ground flaxseed

Juice the grapefruit, pineapple, ginger, and mint leaves, then transfer the juice to a blender. Add the strawberries, oats, flaxseed, and a handful of ice. Blend until smooth.

banana, raspberry & spinach with flaxseed

see variations page 40

Tiny but mighty, flaxseed is not a grain but it is similar to grains in terms of the types of vitamins and minerals it contains. However, the amount of fiber, antioxidants, and omega 3 fatty acids contained in flaxseed leaves grains trailing far behind! It is also thought that flaxseed can help to protect against cancer by interfering with the growth and spread of tumor cells.

1 cup coconut water
2 tsp. ground flaxseed
1/2 cup raspberries
1/2 ripe banana

1 cup baby spinach
4 tsp. smooth peanut butter
1 tsp. green superfood powder
1/2 tsp. lemon juice

Place all the ingredients in a blender with a handful of ice. Blend until smooth.

mango & banana

see variations page 41

The mango contains antioxidants that are said to have powerful anti-cancer properties, and also an enzyme that is purported to be partly responsible for feelings of contentment and for soothing the stomach. The vitamin E in mangoes can help to regulate the body's hormone system, making it perform more efficiently, and it also boosts the libido.

2 fuji or gala apples
1/2 lime, peeled
1/4 cucumber
1 ripe banana

1/2 mango, peeled, pitted, and cubed
1/4 avocado, peeled
1 tsp. wheat germ

Juice the apples, lime, and cucumber, then transfer the juice to a blender with the banana, mango, avocado, and wheat germ. Add a handful of ice. Blend until smooth.

apple & maple starter

see variations page 42

There has been a marked increase in the occurrence of type 2 diabetes in the developed world. Eating apples and other fruits such as blueberries and grapes can reduce the risk of developing type 2 diabetes. This may be due to their beneficial role in blood sugar regulation, as apples contain compounds that are thought to combat the development of diabetes.

3 fuji or gala apples
2 tbsp. quick-cooking rolled oats
1/2 cup almond milk

1 tbsp. maple syrup
1 tsp. wheat germ
1/2 tsp. ground cinnamon

Juice the apples and transfer the juice to a blender. Add the rolled oats, almond milk, maple syrup, wheat germ, cinnamon, and a handful of ice. Blend until smooth.

cranberry & blueberry with oats

see variations page 43

The oats contained in this juice make it an excellent choice for breakfast as they are very filling, and they also help to lower cholesterol. The protein powder will give you plenty of energy, and the cranberries are good for the heart and are known to help lower bad cholesterol levels. They contain citric acid and other nutrients that can aid in the prevention not only of kidney stones, but also other kidney and bladder problems. Consuming cranberries may help to prevent dental disease, cavities, and plaque build-up. Cranberries are also high in antioxidants that will help your body fight off free radicals, which contribute to the aging process.

1 1/4 cups fresh or frozen cranberries
1 large orange, peeled
2 medium carrots
1/2 lime, peeled
1/4 medium pineapple

1/2 cup plain yogurt
1/2 cup blueberries
1 tbsp. quick-cooking rolled oats
1 tbsp. rice or pea protein powder

Juice the cranberries, orange, carrots, lime, and pineapple. Transfer the juice to a blender, add the yogurt, blueberries, quick-cooking oats, rice or pea protein powder, and a handful of ice and blend until smooth.

goji berry wake-up juice

see variations page 44

Goji berries have been used in traditional Chinese medicine for thousands of years, and some people claim they are a natural remedy for diabetes, hypertension, and malaria, although nothing has been proven conclusively. They are a great source of antioxidants and may help to reduce fatigue and stress. You can eat goji berries raw, or soak them in liquid first to rehydrate them—they taste a little herby, with a slight sweetness. Occasionally, they will react with some medicines, so if you are taking any medication, read the accompanying leaflets to check the details before consuming goji berries. Also, if you have pollen allergies or kidney problems, you should avoid goji berries.

1 cup coconut milk
1/2 cup coconut water
2 tbsp. goji berries
1 cup frozen blueberries
1/2 cup frozen raspberries

1/2 cup frozen blackberries
1 tbsp. ground flaxseed
2 tsp. coconut oil
1 tsp. vanilla extract

Put the coconut milk and coconut water in a blender, add the goji berries and leave to soak for 30 minutes. Add the remaining ingredients and blend until smooth. If you use fresh fruit, add a handful of ice before blending.

gooseberry, peach & apple

see variations page 45

Gooseberries are low in calories and they contain significantly high quantities of specific compounds that have numerous health-benefiting effects. These may help to prevent cancer and neurological diseases, alleviate inflammation, and slow down the effects of aging. Gooseberries are rich in potassium, which is good for heart health, and they also help to reduce bad cholesterol and improve nerve health.

1 cup gooseberries
1 fuji or gala apple
1 peach, pitted
1/2 ripe banana

1/4 mango, peeled, pitted, and cubed
1 tbsp. quick-cooking rolled oats
1 tsp. lucuma powder
1 tsp. ground flaxseed

Juice the gooseberries, apple, and peach. Transfer the juice to a blender, add the banana, mango, oats, lucuma powder, ground flaxseed, and a handful of ice. Blend until smooth.

carrot & fennel with maca powder

see variations page 46

Carrots are considered antiaging as their high levels of beta-carotene act as an antioxidant to combat the cell damage that the body experiences due to regular metabolism. Beta-carotene helps to slow down the aging of cells and prevent premature wrinkling, acne, dry skin, blemishes, uneven skin tone, and pigmentation.

2 granny smith apples
2 medium carrots
3 fennel stalks (including fronds)

1/4 cucumber
1/2 cup baby spinach
1 tbsp. maca powder

Juice the apples, carrots, fennel, cucumber, and spinach. Transfer the juice to a blender. Add the maca powder and a handful of ice. Blend until smooth.

chocolate & spinach energy plus

see variations page 47

Spinach is rich in iron, so has remarkable abilities to restore energy, increase vitality, and improve the quality of blood. It is also a good source of manganese, magnesium, folic acid, and vitamins A, B2, C, and K. This drink tastes rich and chocolatey. Don't let the dark green color put you off—it simply indicates that spinach contains high levels of chlorophyll and health-promoting carotenoids, which have anti-inflammatory and anti-cancerous properties. They are especially important for healthy eyesight, helping to prevent macular degeneration and cataracts.

1 1/2 cups coconut milk
1 cup baby spinach
1/2 ripe banana
1 tbsp. unsweetened cocoa powder

2 tsp. green superfood powder
1/2 tsp. guarana
pinch of grated chocolate

Place all the ingredients, except the grated chocolate, in a blender with a handful of ice. Blend until smooth. Sprinkle with a little grated chocolate to decorate.

orange & strawberry with cashew milk

see variations page 48

Cashews have a lower fat content than most other nuts. Approximately 80 percent of their fat is unsaturated fatty acids. Plus, about 66 percent of this unsaturated fatty acid content is made up of heart-healthy monounsaturated fats, similar to those found in olive oil. They also contain copper, which is good for the body's antioxidant defenses and energy production, and for healthy bones and blood vessels. Cashews contain magnesium, which is also good for healthy bones, and nuts are useful for reducing the risk of developing gallstones.

cashew milk
2/3 cup raw cashew nuts
1 1/2 cups water
1 tsp. maple syrup (or agave syrup)
1/2 tsp. vanilla extract
1/4 tsp. sea salt

juice
1 fuji or gala apple
1 cup baby spinach
1 medium orange, peeled
1 cup cashew milk
1 3/4 cups hulled strawberries
1/2 ripe banana
1 tbsp. quick-cooking rolled oats
1 tsp. protein powder

First make the cashew milk. Soak the cashew nuts in water for about 4 hours, then rinse until the water runs clear. Put the soaked cashew nuts in a blender and add the water. Blend on a low setting at first, then increase the speed until the cashew nuts are pulverized and the liquid is smooth. Add the maple syrup (or agave syrup), vanilla extract, and sea salt and

then pulse again. This should make about 2 cups of cashew milk. You will need 1 cup for the juice—you can store the remainder in the refrigerator in an airtight container for 3–4 days.

Juice the apple, spinach, and orange. Transfer the juice to a blender, add 1 cup cashew milk, the strawberries, banana, oats, protein powder, and a handful of ice. Blend until smooth.

coconut, banana, maca & chia shake

see variations page 49

This juice contains both maca powder and chia seeds. Maca is a root that belongs to the radish family and is most commonly found in powder form. It is grown in the mountains of Peru and has been called Peruvian ginseng. It has recently become popular as a health supplement and food ingredient. While no serious known side effects are evident, as with any other supplement, it should not be taken in large amounts. It is recommended that you should start with 1/2 teaspoon per day and build up slowly. Do not take more than 1 tablespoon as a daily dose, and alternate a few days on and a few days off. Maca powder contains many vitamins and minerals, and athletes often take it for optimum performance. It can help to boost the libido and alleviate womens' menstrual and menopausal symptoms.

1 cup coconut milk
1 tbsp. chia seeds
1 ripe banana
1/4 mango, peeled, pitted, and cubed

4 tbsp. coconut water
1 tbsp. coconut oil
1 tbsp. honey
1/2 tsp. maca powder

Put the coconut milk and chia seeds in a blender and leave to soak for 30 minutes. Add the remaining ingredients with a handful of ice. Blend until smooth.

blueberry & cherry

see base recipe page 17

blueberry, cherry & prune juice
Omit the acai juice and plain yogurt and substitute prune juice and blueberry-flavored Greek-style yogurt.

blueberry & chocolate cherry juice with flaxseed
Add 2 teaspoons cacao powder and 1 tablespoon ground flaxseed to the blender with the rest of the ingredients.

blueberry & cherry antioxidant juice with added protein & guarana
Omit the quick-cooking oats and add 2 teaspoons pea or rice protein powder and 1/2 teaspoon guarana.

dairy-free blueberry, coconut & cherry antioxidant juice
Omit the yogurt, substituting 1/2 cup dairy-free coconut yogurt or coconut milk, and add 2 tablespoons unsweetened flaked coconut.

variations

breakfast berries

see base recipe page 18

breakfast berries with almonds
Omit the flaxseed, ground ginger, and milk. Add 1 tablespoon ground almonds to the blender along with 1 cup almond milk and 1 teaspoon honey.

breakfast berries with blueberries & blackberries
Omit the milk, 1/3 cup of the raspberries, 1/2 cup of the strawberries, and the ginger. Add 1/4 cup each of blueberries and blackberries to the blender with 1/2 cup plain yogurt and 1 teaspoon vanilla extract.

breakfast berry blend with banana & vanilla
Omit the ground ginger. Add 1 teaspoon vanilla extract and 1/2 ripe banana to the blender.

dairy-free breakfast berry & orange blend
Juice 1/2 large orange with the apple and pineapple. Omit the whole milk, substituting coconut milk.

variations

spicy grapefruit & strawberry juice with mint

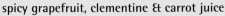

see base recipe page 21

spicy grapefruit, clementine & carrot juice
Juice the grapefruit with 1 peeled clementine, 2 carrots, and 1 cup baby spinach, then blend the juice with the oats, flaxseed, and ice, omitting the ginger, mint, and strawberries, until smooth.

spicy grapefruit, strawberry & melon juice
Add 1 cup chopped melon to the blender with the rest of the ingredients.

spicy grapefruit & strawberry juice with basil
Omit the mint and substitute 4 basil leaves.

spicy grapefruit & strawberry juice with black pepper
Omit the mint and substitute 1/4 teaspoon freshly ground black pepper.

variations

banana, raspberry & spinach with flaxseed

see base recipe page 22

banana, strawberry & spinach with spirulina
Omit the raspberries and substitute 1 cup strawberries. Add 1 teaspoon spirulina to the blender with the rest of the ingredients.

banana, raspberry & kale with almonds
Omit the spinach and peanut butter. Juice 1 cup kale and add the juice to the blender with 1 tablespoon ground almonds and the rest of the ingredients.

banana, raspberry, melon & spinach with flaxseed
Add 1 cup cubed melon to the blender with the rest of the ingredients.

banana, blueberry & peach with flaxseed
Omit the spinach and peanut butter and add 2 tablespoons blueberries and 2 ripe peaches, pitted and chopped, to the blender with the rest of the ingredients.

mango & banana

see base recipe page 24

mango & banana with orange & strawberry
Omit 1 apple, the lime and the avocado. Juice 2 medium oranges with the apple and cucumber, then transfer to the blender with the banana, mango, wheat germ, 1 3/4 cups hulled strawberries, 2 tablespoons plain yogurt, and the ice.

mango & banana with oatmeal & almonds
Omit the wheat germ. Substitute 1 tablespoon quick-cooking oats and add 2 teaspoons ground almonds.

mango, banana & pineapple juice blend
Omit the apples and avocado. Juice 1/4 large pineapple with the lime and cucumber. Add 1 teaspoon honey and 2 tablespoons plain yogurt to the blender with the juice and the remaining ingredients.

mango, banana & peanut butter
Omit the avocado and wheat germ. Add 1 tablespoon smooth peanut butter and 2 tablespoons plain yogurt to the blender.

variations

apple & maple starter

see base recipe page 25

apple & maple starter with blackberries

After juicing the apples, pack 1 cup blackberries tightly into the funnel of the juicer and juice on slow speed. Transfer the juice to the blender and continue with the recipe.

apple, pineapple & maple starter

Juice 1/4 medium pineapple and 1/4 medium cucumber with the apples, then continue as per the base recipe.

apple & blueberry starter with honey

Substitute whole milk for the almond milk, and add 2 tablespoons blueberries and 2 tablespoons plain yogurt. Omit the maple syrup and substitute 1 teaspoon honey to the blender with the rest of the ingredients.

apple & lemon starter with cucumber & ginger

Omit the almond milk, maple syrup, wheat germ, and ground cinnamon. Juice a 1/2-in. (1-cm) slice of lemon with the peel on, a 1-in. (2.5-cm) slice of cucumber, a 1-in. (2.5-cm) piece of celery stalk and a 1/2-in. (1-cm) piece fresh gingerroot with the apples. Blend with the oats, and a handful of ice, until smooth.

apple & maple starter with banana

Add 1/2 ripe banana to the blender with the rest of the ingredients.

cranberry & blueberry with oats

see base recipe page 27

cranberry & apple with oatmeal
Substitute 2 apples for the orange.

cranberry & blackberry with hemp protein
Substitute blackberries for blueberries, and hemp protein for the pea protein.

cranberry & mango with oatmeal
Omit the blueberries and substitute 1/2 mango, peeled and pitted.

dairy-free cranberry & blueberry with oatmeal
Omit the plain yogurt and substitute coconut yogurt or coconut milk.

variations

goji berry wake-up juice

see base recipe page 28

goji berry & beet wake-up juice

Juice 1 medium raw beet. Follow the basic recipe and, after the goji berries have soaked, add the beet juice to the blender with the rest of the ingredients.

goji berry & kiwi fruit wake-up juice

Omit 1/2 cup coconut milk and the vanilla extract. Increase the coconut water to 1 cup. Add 2 peeled kiwifruit to the blender with the rest of the ingredients.

goji berry & orange wake-up juice

Juice 2 peeled oranges and substitute the juice for the coconut milk.

goji berry & carrot wake-up juice

Juice 1 large orange and 3 carrots and substitute the juice for the coconut milk.

gooseberry, peach & apple

see base recipe page 30

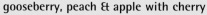

gooseberry, peach & apple with cherry
Juice 1 1/4 cups pitted cherries with the gooseberries, apple, and peach.

gooseberry, peach & apple with avocado
Omit the banana, substituting 1/2 avocado.

gooseberry, peach & apple with fig
Omit the mango, and juice 2 figs with the gooseberries, apple, and peach.

gooseberry, peach & apple with blackberry
Omit the mango. Add 1/2 cup blackberries to the blender with the rest of the ingredients.

variations

carrot & fennel with maca powder

see base recipe page 31

carrot, mango & maca powder
Omit the fennel. Add 1/2 mango, peeled and pitted, to the blender with the juice and maca powder.

carrot, banana & maca powder
Omit the fennel. Add 1/2 banana to the blender with the juice and maca powder.

carrot, avocado & maca powder
Omit the fennel. Add 1/2 avocado, peeled and pitted, to the blender with the juice and maca powder.

carrot, pineapple & maca powder
Omit the fennel, juicing 1/4 medium pineapple with the apples, carrots, cucumber, and spinach.

chocolate & almond energy plus

see base recipe page 33

mocha almond protein plus
Add 1 teaspoon instant coffee powder to the blender with the rest of the ingredients.

chocolate, orange & almond protein plus
Juice 1 medium peeled orange and add the juice to the blender with 1/2 cup almond milk and the rest of the ingredients.

chocolate & avocado protein plus
Omit the banana, substituting 1/2 avocado, peeled and pitted.

chocolate & apricot protein plus
Add 2 pitted apricots to the blender with the rest of the ingredients.

variations

orange & strawberry with cashew milk

see base recipe page 34

orange, almond & raspberry
Omit the cashew milk and strawberries. Substitute almond milk and raspberries. Add 1 tablespoon almond butter to the blender with the rest of the ingredients.

orange, cashew & blueberry
Omit the strawberries, substituting blueberries. Add 1 tablespoon cashew butter to the blender with the rest of the ingredients.

orange, coconut & strawberry
Prepare the basic recipe, substituting coconut milk for the cashew milk, and adding 1 tablespoon unsweetened coconut flakes to the blender with the rest of the ingredients.

variations

coconut, banana, maca & chia shake

see base recipe page 36

banana, blueberry & wheat germ shake
Omit the chia seeds and mango. Add 1 tablespoon wheat germ and 1/2 cup blueberries to the blender with the rest of the ingredients, and blend as before.

banana, pineapple, cacao, maca & chia shake
Omit the mango. Juice 1/4 medium pineapple and add the juice to the blender with 1 tablespoon cacao powder and the rest of the ingredients.

banana, papaya, oat maca & chia shake
Omit the mango and substitute 1/4 papaya, peeled, seeded, and cubed. Add 1 tablespoon quick-cooking oats to the blender with the rest of the ingredients.

banana, fig, coconut, maca & chia shake
Omit the mango. Juice 2 fresh figs and add the juice to the blender with the rest of the ingredients.

fruit &
vegetable mixes

One of the easiest ways to get your five-a-day is in a glass. In fact, ensuring you've had all five becomes quite an effortless task. In this chapter you'll find recipes for fabulous mixes of fruits and vegetables. Each of these pack a nutritional punch, with a mighty amount of goodness condensed into a glass.

apple, pear, carrot, & cucumber

see variations page 74

Pears are often recommended as a hypo-allergenic fruit, which means that they are less likely to produce adverse allergic reactions. Pear juice is safe to give to infants as pears are mild, yet very good for you. They contain potassium, which helps your heart beat normally, and to keep your muscles working the way they should. It also has vitamins C, K, and A, for preventing infection, keeping the immune system strong, and maintaining eye health.

2 medium carrots
1 fuji or gala apple
1 pear
1/2 raw beet

1 stalk of celery
1/4 cucumber
1/2-in. (1-cm) piece fresh gingerroot
1/2 mango, peeled, pitted, and cubed

Juice the carrots, apple, pear, beet, celery, cucumber, and ginger. Transfer the juice to a blender with the mango and a handful of ice. Blend until smooth.

leafy pineapple power juice

see variations page 75

Dark green leafy vegetables, such as spinach, cabbage, kale, broccoli, and chard, are all high in iron. Vegetarians, people with iron-deficiency anemia, and pregnant women are all encouraged to include green leafy vegetables as part of a balanced diet. Green superfood powder contains a well-balanced organic mix of nutritionally super-dense dehydrated grass and vegetable extracts (wheat grass, barley grass, alfalfa, spirulina, blue-green algae, spinach, and broccoli), and just 1 teaspoon will give you an amazing boost of energy.

2 fuji or gala apples
2 cups baby spinach
3 1/2 cups Swiss chard
1/4 cucumber

1/4 medium pineapple
1/4 lime, peeled
1 tsp. green superfood powder

Place 1 apple in the funnel of the juicer and pack the greens on top. Then add the other apple and the cucumber, and juice the lot. Add the pineapple and lime to the funnel and juice. Transfer the juice to a blender with the superfood powder and a handful of ice, and blend until smooth. If it separates, stir just before serving.

apple, kiwi & carrot

see variations page 76

The old saying that carrots are good for the eyes is one of the few that we got right. They are rich in beta-carotene, which is converted into vitamin A in the liver. Vitamin A is transformed in the retina to rhodopsin, a purple pigment necessary for night vision. Beta-carotene has also been shown to protect against macular degeneration.

2 granny smith apples
1/2 kiwifruit, peeled
2 large carrots

1/2 cup fresh curly parsley
1 stalk of celery

Juice all the ingredients and pour over ice to serve.

beet & orange with honey & acai

see variations page 77

Acai berries are classed as a superfood because they contain superior nutritional value for the amount of calories they have. They not only have a high concentration of antioxidants, but they also contain fiber to aid digestion, lots of different vitamins, and they are naturally high in essential fatty acids, which is great for heart health.

1 medium raw beet
2 medium oranges, peeled
2 dark red plums, pitted

1/2 cup whole milk
1 tbsp. acai powder
1 tbsp. honey

Juice the beet, oranges, and plums, then transfer the juice to a blender. Add the milk, acai powder, honey, and a handful of ice. Blend until smooth.

apple, parsley & cucumber

see variations page 78

Parsley is one of the world's most popular herbs, and it is highly nutritious so provides much more than decoration. It promotes bladder health and contains two types of unusual components that provide unique health benefits — volatile oil components and flavonoids. In animal studies these components have been shown to inhibit tumor formation, particularly in the lungs.

2 fuji or gala apples
large handful of fresh parsley
1/2 cucumber

1 lime, peeled
1 tsp. virgin coconut oil
1/3 cup coconut water

Juice the apples, parsley, cucumber, and lime. Transfer the juice to a blender and add the coconut oil, coconut water, and a handful of ice. Blend until smooth.

pineapple, strawberry & cucumber

see variations page 79

The cucumber is one of the oldest cultivated crops and is considered a superfood for its effects on overall health. Good for digestive problems and very low in calories, it has healing attributes in relation to diseases of both the bladder and kidney. Considered a diuretic, it has been suggested that regular consumption of cucumber can dissolve kidney stones over time. It also contains an enzyme called erepsin, which aids in the digestion of protein and in turn may improve energy levels.

1/4 pineapple
1 fuji or gala apple
1/2 cucumber

1/2 lime, peeled
3 1/4 cups hulled strawberries
1 tsp. wheat germ

Juice the pineapple, apple, cucumber, and lime. Transfer the juice to a blender and add the strawberries, wheat germ, and a handful of ice. Blend until smooth.

fennel, pineapple & celery

see variations page 80

Fennel is closely related to parsley, carrots, and cilantro. It blends well with other foods, enhancing their flavors. It was held in high esteem in Roman medicine over 2,000 years ago, and was used to enhance longevity, strength, and courage. Fennel has amazingly diverse health benefits, including relief from anemia, indigestion, bloating, flatulence, constipation, colic, diarrhea, respiratory disorders, and menstrual symptoms, and can also help with upper respiratory infections.

1 fuji or gala apple
1/4 pineapple
3 fennel stalks (with fronds)

2 stalks of celery
1/2-in. (1-cm) piece fresh gingerroot

Juice the apple, pineapple, fennel, celery, and ginger. Pour over ice to serve.

cabbage, mango & blueberry with a kick

see variations page 81

This juice packs a massive punch on the health front. Mangoes are not only one of the sweetest fruits in the world, but are full of vitamins, minerals, and antioxidants. They contain beta-carotene, vitamin E, and selenium, which can all help to guard against heart disease and other illnesses such as colon and cervical cancer. Mangoes also contain vitamins A and C, making them a great source of potassium, which helps to regulate blood pressure and muscle contractions, and keep bodily processes working correctly.

2 1/2 cups chopped cabbage leaves
2 fuji or gala apples
1/2 lemon, peeled
1/2 mango, peeled, pitted, and cubed

3/4 cup blueberries
1/4 avocado, peeled
1 tbsp. ground flaxseed
1/4 tsp. cayenne pepper

Juice the cabbage, apples, and lemon. Transfer the juice to a blender and add the mango, blueberries, avocado, flaxseed, cayenne pepper, and a handful of ice. Blend until smooth.

cranberry & celery cleanser

see variations page 82

Native Americans treated a variety of illnesses—including bladder infections—with cranberry preparations. We now know that this would have been effective because compounds in cranberries may actually hinder bacteria from attaching to the lining of the bladder. Besides being high in antioxidants, cranberries are a rich source of the flavonoid quercetin, which may inhibit the development of both breast and colon cancer. Cranberries are high in vitamin C and also have other anti-inflammatory effects that are important for disease prevention.

2 fuji or gala apples
1 pear
1 1/2 cups baby spinach
1/2 cup fresh or frozen cranberries

1/2 stalk of celery
1/4 cucumber
1/4 avocado, peeled
1 tsp. ground flaxseed

Juice the apples, pear, spinach, cranberries, celery, and cucumber. Transfer the juice to a blender and add the avocado and ground flaxseed. Blend until smooth. Pour over ice to serve.

mint, apple & lettuce leaf energiser

see variations page 83

Mint is not only a great palate cleanser and appetizer, but it also promotes digestion and soothes stomachs in cases of indigestion or inflammation. As it is a naturally soothing substance, the strong and refreshing aroma of mint offers a quick and effective remedy for nausea, and it can alleviate the inflammation that is often associated with headaches and migraines. Mint can be effective in providing relief for respiratory disorders such as asthma and the common cold, and it can also sooth the throat and relieve irritation, which causes chronic coughing.

2 granny smith apples
1/4 cucumber
3 cups lettuce leaves

8 fresh mint leaves
1/3 cup raspberries
1/2 cup coconut water

Juice the apples, cucumber, lettuce leaves, and mint. Transfer the juice to a blender and add the raspberries, coconut water, and a handful of ice. Blend until smooth.

beet & ginger lemon applechia

see variations page 84

Beet is high in many nutrients, including vitamins A, B, and C, potassium, magnesium, fiber, phosphorus, iron, beta-carotene, betacyanin, and folic acid. It is a wonderful tonic for the liver as it works as a purifier for the blood, and can help to prevent various forms of cancer. Beet can also help your mental health as it contains betaine, which is the same substance that is used in certain treatments for depression, and trytophan, which relaxes the mind, lowers blood pressure, and creates a sense of well-being.

1 cup coconut water
1 tbsp. chia seeds
2 fuji or gala apples
2 1/2 cups fresh parsley

2 small raw beets
2 lemons, peeled
1-in. (2.5-cm) piece fresh gingerroot

Put the coconut water in a blender, add the chia seeds and leave to soak for 30 minutes.

Put the apples in the funnel of the juicer, pack the parsley on top, and finish with the beets, lemons, ginger, and juice the mixture.

Put the juice into the blender with the soaked chia seeds, blend until smooth, then pour over ice to serve.

orange & pear with spinach, cucumber & pumpkin seeds

see variations page 85

Pumpkin seeds are concentrated sources of many health-benefiting vitamins, minerals, antioxidants, and all-important essential amino acids. They contain magnesium for a healthy heart, tryptophan for restful sleep, zinc for immune support, and they have anti-inflammatory benefits. They are good for prostate health, are rich in healthy fats that provide benefits for heart and liver health, and some studies suggest they may help improve insulin regulation.

1 pear
1 orange, peeled
1/2 lime, peeled
1 cup baby spinach
1/2 cucumber

1/2 ripe banana
4 tbsp. coconut water
1 tbsp. pumpkin seeds, chopped
1 tsp. green superfood powder
1 tsp. virgin coconut oil

Put the pear, orange and lime in the funnel of the juicer, pack the spinach on top, finish with the cucumber, and juice the mixture.

Transfer the juice to a blender, add the banana, coconut water, pumpkin seeds, superfood powder, coconut oil and a handful of ice. Blend until smooth.

melon, pear & sweet potato

see variations page 86

Melons are highly underrated, especially as they contain antioxidants, vitamins and minerals that help to prevent many common health problems such as cancers, birth defects and high blood pressure. They contain an anticoagulant that helps to prevent stroke and heart disease. Melons also contain collagen, which affects the integrity of the cell structure in all connective tissue, such as skin.

2 pears
1 small sweet potato (skin on)
1/2 small melon, peeled, seeded, and cubed

Juice the pears and sweet potato.

Transfer the juice to a blender with the melon and a handful of ice. Blend until smooth.

zucchini, beet, cabbage & pear

see variations page 87

Zucchinis are not a powerhouse of micro-nutrients, but they do have some very valuable qualities in terms of cancer prevention. Research has shown that squashes in general, including zucchinis, have properties that inhibit cell mutations and prevent colon and lung cancer. The zucchini is rich in magnesium and potassium, which are good for heart health, regulating blood pressure and controlling blood glucose levels.

2 pears
1 medium raw beet
3/4 cup chopped green cabbage
1 tomato

1 lemon, peeled
1/2 zucchini
1/2-in. (1-cm) piece fresh gingerroot

Juice all the ingredients and serve over ice.

apple, pear, carrot & cucumber

see base recipe page 51

apple, blackberry, carrot & zucchini
Omit the pear and celery, substituting 1/2 cup blackberries (juicing on a slow speed) and 1/4 zucchini when juicing.

orange, pear, avocado & cucumber
Omit the apple and carrot, substituting 1 peeled medium orange when juicing. Add 1/4 avocado, peeled, to the blender with the rest of the ingredients.

apple, pear, blueberry & cucumber
Omit the carrot, beet, and ginger. Instead, juice 1/2 cup blueberries with the apple, pear, celery, and cucumber.

orange, cranberry, carrot & cucumber
Omit the apple and pear. Substitute 1 medium peeled orange and 3/4 cup cranberries when juicing.

variations

leafy pineapple power juice

see base recipe page 52

leafy pineapple power juice with peanut butter
Omit the chard. Add 1/3 cup coconut milk to the blender with the juice and ice, along with 1 tablespoon smooth peanut butter.

leafy pineapple power shake with avocado
Omit the chard. Add 4 tablespoons plain yogurt and 1/4 avocado to the blender with the juice and ice.

leafy pineapple power juice with avocado
Omit the chard. Add 1/4 avocado to the blender with the juice and ice.

leafy pineapple power juice with beet
Omit the chard, substituting 1 medium raw beet.

apple, kiwi & carrot

see base recipe page 55

apple, kiwi & mango
Omit the carrots when juicing. Place 1/2 mango, peeled, pitted, and cubed, in a blender with the juice and a handful of ice. Blend until smooth.

apple, kiwi & peaches
Omit the carrots when juicing. Put 2 ripe pitted peaches in a blender with the juice, and a handful of ice. Blend until smooth.

apple, kiwi & carrot with tahini
Omit the parsley and celery when juicing, substituting 1/4 pineapple, and 1/4 cucumber. Transfer the juice to a blender with 1 tablespoon tahini, and a handful of ice and blend until smooth.

apple, kiwi & carrot with almond butter
Prepare the basic recipe, then transfer the juice to a blender with 1 tablespoon almond butter, 1 tablespoon ground almonds, and 4 tablespoons almond milk. Add a handful of ice and blend until smooth.

beet & orange with honey & acai

see base recipe page 56

beet & orange with honey & spirulina
Prepare the basic recipe, omitting the acai powder and substituting 1 teaspoon spirulina.
Blend as before.

beet & apple with spinach & blackberry
Omit the oranges and milk. Juice 2 fuji or gala apples and 1 cup baby spinach with the beet
and plums. Add 1/2 cup blackberries with the acai powder, honey, and ice.

beet & orange with figs
Omit the plums when juicing, substituting 2 fresh figs.

dairy-free beet & orange with honey & agave
Omit the milk and honey, substituting almond milk and agave syrup.

variations

apple, parsley & cucumber

see base recipe page 58

apple, watercress & cucumber
Omit the parsley, substituting watercress.

apple, mint & cucumber
Omit the parsley, substituting 8 mint leaves.

apple, kale & cucumber
Omit the parsley, substituting kale.

apple, parsley & celery
Omit the cucumber, substituting 3 stalks of celery.

variations

pineapple, strawberry & cucumber

see base recipe page 59

pineapple, black currant & strawberry
Prepare the basic recipe, adding 1/2 cup black currants to the juicer with the pineapple, apple, cucumber, and lime.

pineapple, strawberry & carrot
Add 2 medium carrots to the juicer with the pineapple, apple, cucumber, and lime.

pineapple, strawberry & broccoli
Add 5 small broccoli florets to the juicer with the pineapple, apple, cucumber, and lime.

Pineapple, strawberry & cucumber with cilantro
Add a handful of cilantro to the juicer with the pineapple, apple, cucumber, and lime.

variations

fennel, pineapple & celery

see base recipe page 61

fennel, pineapple & cucumber
Prepare the basic recipe, omitting the celery and substituting 1/2 cucumber.

fennel, pineapple & lettuce
Omit the celery, substituting 3 cups lettuce leaves.

fennel, pineapple, lime & basil
Add 1/4 peeled lime and a few fresh basil leaves to the juicer with the rest of the ingredients.

fennel, pineapple, carrot & ginger
Add 1 medium carrot and 1/4-in. (5-mm) piece fresh gingerroot to the juicer with the rest of the ingredients.

cabbage, mango & blueberry with a kick

see base recipe page 62

cabbage, papaya & blackberry with a kick
Omit the mango and blueberries and substitute 1/2 papaya, peeled and seeded, and blackberries.

kale, mango & black currant with a kick
Substitute kale for the cabbage and black currants for the blueberries.

lettuce, mango & blueberry with a kick
Substitute 3 cups lettuce leaves for the cabbage.

spinach, mango & plums with lavender
Omit the cabbage, blueberries, and cayenne pepper. Substitute baby spinach for the cabbage and juice 3 pitted plums with the apples and lemon. Add 1 teaspoon crushed dried lavender leaves to the blender with the rest of the ingredients.

cranberry & celery cleanser

see base recipe page 64

cranberry & celery cleanser with dandelion

Prepare the basic recipe, adding 4 dandelion leaves to the juicer with the rest of the ingredients.

cranberry & celery cleanser with spirulina

Add 1/2 teaspoon spirulina to the blender with the rest of the ingredients.

cranberry & celery cleanser with peaches

Omit the apples, substituting 2 pitted peaches.

cranberry & celery cleanser with goji berries

Add 1 tablespoon goji berries to the blender with the juice. Leave to soak for 30 minutes, then add the rest of the ingredients and a handful of ice. Blend until smooth.

mint, apple & lettuce leaf energiser

see base recipe page 65

mint, apple & blackberry energiser
Prepare the basic recipe, omitting the cucumber and raspberries. Add 1/4 melon, cubed, and 1/2 cup blackberries to the blender with the rest of the ingredients.

mint, apple & spinach energizer with plums & guarana
Substitute 1 cup baby spinach for the lettuce leaves. Omit the raspberries and juice 2 pitted plums with the apples, cucumber, spinach and mint. Add 1/2 teaspoon guarana to the blender with the rest of the ingredients.

mint, apple & kale energiser with figs & protein powder
Omit the lettuce leaves, substituting 1 cup kale. Omit the raspberries and juice 2 figs with the apples, cucumber, kale, and mint. Add 1 teaspoon protein powder to the blender with the rest of the ingredients.

mint, apple & watercress with blueberries
Omit the lettuce leaves, substituting 2 cups watercress. Substitute blueberries for the raspberries.

variations

beet & ginger lemon applechia

see base recipe page 67

beet & ginger grapefruit applechia
Prepare the basic recipe, omitting the lemons and substituting 1 large pink grapefuit, peeled.

beet & ginger gooseberry applechia
Omit the lemons, substituting 1 cup gooseberries.

beet & ginger orange applechia
Omit the lemons, substituting 2 medium oranges, peeled.

beet & ginger rhubarb applechia
Omit the lemons, substituting 2 1/4 cups chopped rhubarb.

variations

orange & pear with spinach, cucumber, & pumpkin seeds

see base recipe page 68

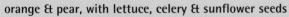

orange & pear, with lettuce, celery & sunflower seeds
Prepare the basic recipe, substituting 1 1/2 cups lettuce leaves for the spinach,
2 stalks of celery for the cucumber, and sunflower seeds for the pumpkin seeds.

orange & pear, with kale, broccoli & poppy seeds
Substitute kale for the spinach, broccoli for the cucumber and poppy seeds for the
pumpkin seeds.

orange & pear, with cabbage, zucchini & walnuts
Prepare the basic recipe, substituting cabbage leaves for the spinach, 1 1/4 cups
chopped zucchini for the cucumber, and 1 tablespoon finely chopped walnuts for
the pumpkin seeds.

orange & pear, with sweet potato, carrots & cilantro
Omit the spinach, cucumber and pumpkin seeds. Juice 1/2 small sweet potato and
1 large carrot with the pear, orange and lime. Add 1 tablespoon freshly chopped
cilantro to the blender with the rest of the ingredients.

variations

melon, pear & sweet potato

see base recipe page 71

melon, pear & butternut squash with plums
Prepare the basic recipe, omitting the sweet potato and substituting 1 3/4 cups cubed butternut squash and 2 pitted plums.

melon, apple & carrot
Omit the sweet potato, substituting 2 medium carrots.

melon, prunes & sweet potato
Add 1/2 cup canned prunes, drained and pitted, to the blender with the rest of the ingredients.

melon, peach & sweet potato
Omit the pears, substituting 3 pitted peaches.

zucchini, beet, cabbage & pear

see base recipe page 72

zucchini, beet, cabbage & orange
Omit the pears and lemon and substitute 1 apple and 1 orange, peeled.

zucchini, beet, spinach & grapefruit
Omit the cabbage and lemon and substitute 1 cup baby spinach and 1 pink grapefruit, peeled.

zucchini, beet, watercress & rhubarb
Substitute 1 1/3 cups watercress for the cabbage and 2 1/4 cups chopped rhubarb for the pears.

zucchini, beet, lettuce & gooseberries
Omit the cabbage and pears, substituting 3 cups lettuce leaves and 1 cup gooseberries.

kid friendly

This chapter is full of ideas for juices that children
in particular will find appealing. These recipes are
a little on the sweet side, or are made using familiar
flavors, and some are reminiscent of favorite
desserts, to be extra tempting!

apple pie delight

see variations page 108

Apple consumption is associated with a lower risk of death from both coronary heart disease and cardiovascular disease. Finnish researchers studying dietary data collected over 28 years from 9,208 men and women found that frequent apple eaters had the lowest risk of suffering strokes compared with non-apple eaters. Experts attribute the heart-healthy benefits to antioxidant compounds found in apples, which help prevent LDL cholesterol from oxidizing and inhibit inflammation. Plus, the soluble fiber in apples has also been shown to reduce cholesterol levels.

2 fuji or gala apples
1/2 ripe banana
4 tbsp. plain or vanilla yogurt
4 tbsp. whole milk

1 tbsp. honey
1/4 tsp. ground cinnamon
1/2 tsp. vanilla extract

Juice the apples and transfer the juice to a blender. Add the banana, yogurt, milk, honey, cinnamon, vanilla extract, and a handful of ice. Blend until smooth.

chocolate peanut butter after-school reviver

see variations page 109

Bananas are rich in vitamin B6, which helps to protect against type 2 diabetes, and to strengthen the nervous system. It also helps with the production of white blood cells. The iron in bananas strengthens the blood and can help to relieve anemia. High in potassium and low in salt, bananas are officially recognized by the FDA as being able to lower blood pressure and protect against heart disease and strokes. Containing pectin, bananas are a natural antacid, they aid digestion and are soothing on the tummy by coating the lining of the stomach against corrosive acids.

2 fuji or gala apples
1/2 cup whole milk
1/2 ripe banana
1 tbsp. natural smooth peanut butter

2 tsp. wheat germ
2 tsp. quick-cooking rolled oats
1 tsp. cacao powder
1/2 tsp. vanilla extract

Juice the apples and transfer the juice to the blender. Add the milk, banana, peanut butter, wheat germ, rolled oats, cacao powder, vanilla extract, and a handful of ice. Blend until smooth.

deconstructed pumpkin pie juice

see variations page 110

Pumpkins are a low-calorie vegetable rich in minerals like copper, calcium, potassium, and phosphorus. They contain dietary fiber, antioxidants, and natural poly-phenolic flavonoid compounds, which convert into vitamin A inside the body. Pumpkins contain no saturated fats or cholesterol, and are one of the food items recommended by dieticians in cholesterol-controlling and weight-reduction programs. Pumpkins are an excellent source of zea-xanthin, which is a natural antioxidant with UV (ultra-violet) ray filtering actions in the retina, meaning that pumpkins can provide some protection from age-related macular disease.

1 gala or fuji apple
1/2 mango, peeled, pitted, and cubed
4 tbsp. pumpkin purée
1/2 ripe banana

1/4 tsp. ground cinnamon
pinch of ground nutmeg
pinch of ground allspice
pinch of ground cloves

Juice the apple and mango. Transfer the juice to a blender with the pumpkin purée, banana, cinnamon, nutmeg, allspice, and ground cloves. Add a handful of ice. Blend until smooth. If desired, grate a little extra nutmeg on top to serve.

lemonade zinger

see variations page 111

Grapes are a sweet fruit, generally loved by children. They are rich in a powerful antioxidant that has been found to play a protective role against viral and fungal infections, many cancers, coronary heart disease, degenerative nerve disease, and Alzheimer's. Grapes are also a rich source of micronutrient minerals like copper, iron, and manganese, and contain vitamins C, A, and K, carotenes, and B-complex vitamins.

3 fuji or gala apples
8 red grapes
1 medium carrot

2 lemons, peeled
1/2-in. (1-cm) piece fresh gingerroot, peeled
4 tbsp. soda water (optional)

Juice the apples, grapes, carrot, lemons, and ginger, and pour over ice to serve. If desired, top with the soda water.

black currant & banana

see variations page 112

Black currants are full of antioxidants called anthocyanins, which give the fruits their distinctive dark purple color. The darker the black currants, the more anthocyanins they contain. They are especially rich in vitamin C, containing more than three times as much as oranges, and they can help to prevent joint inflammation, eye strain, and urinary infections. Adding yogurt to juice for children not only adds calcium, but makes it look like a milkshake, which gives it extra appeal.

2 fuji or gala apples
1 cup fresh or frozen black currants

1 small ripe banana
2 tbsp. plain or vanilla yogurt

Juice the apples and black currants. Transfer the juice to a blender with the banana and yogurt and blend with a handful of ice until smooth.

pineapple & chocolate

see variations page 113

Pineapple is sweet, delicious, refreshing, and a nutrition powerhouse. It is free of cholesterol and fat and is loaded with vitamins and minerals, including vitamins A and C, calcium, phosphorus, and potassium. Pineapples help to build and maintain strong bones because they contain manganese, which is a trace mineral that the body needs in order to build bones and connective tissues. They also contribute to strengthening gums to keep teeth healthy and strong.

2 gala or fuji apples
1/4 large pineapple
2 tsp. unsweetened cocoa powder

Juice the apples and pineapple and transfer the juice to a blender. Add the unsweetened cocoa powder and a handful of ice. Blend until smooth.

apple & orange with kiwi fruit & banana

see variations page 114

Orange trees are the most cultivated fruit trees in the world. The fruit they bear is popular because of its natural sweetness and wide diversity of uses, from juices and marmalades to face masks and candied orange slices. An orange has over 170 different phytochemicals and more than sixty different flavonoids, many of which have been shown to have anti-inflammatory and strong antioxidant effects.

2 small oranges, peeled
1 kiwi fruit, peeled
1 fuji or gala apple

1 ripe banana
4 tbsp. coconut or rice milk
1/2 tsp. vanilla extract

Juice the oranges, kiwi fruit, and apple and transfer the juice to a blender. Add the banana, coconut or rice milk, and vanilla extract and blend with a handful of ice until smooth. Sprinkle with grated orange zest to serve.

carrot cake juicy gem

see variations page 115

Buttermilk has a tart flavor and is full of essential nutrients. It is made by adding cultured bacteria to low-fat or fat-free milk, as with yogurt. The live cultures give it the distinctive rich and creamy texture, and also a lot of health benefits. Buttermilk is high in potassium, vitamin B-12, calcium, and riboflavin. It is also a good source of phosphorus, and those with digestive problems are often advised to choose buttermilk rather than milk, as it is more easily digested. The reduced-fat version still has all the bone-building calcium that is in full-fat buttermilk, but with fewer calories and less fat.

1 fuji or gala apple
2 medium carrots
1/4 pineapple
1/2 cup low-fat buttermilk
1/2 ripe banana
1 tsp. rice or pea protein powder

1 tbsp. quick-cooking rolled oats
2 tsp. ground flaxseed
1/4 tsp. ground ginger
1/4 tsp. ground cinnamon
1/4 tsp. ground allspice

Juice the apple, carrots, and pineapple, then transfer the juice to a blender. Add the remaining ingredients with a handful of ice. Blend until smooth.

chia chocolate coconut protein rush

see variations page 116

Chia seeds are one of the richest plant-based sources of omega-3 fatty acids, and in particular, alpha-linolenic acid. This can help to reduce inflammation, enhance cognitive performance, and reduce bad cholesterol. They also contain antioxidants that help protect the body from free radicals, early aging, and cancer. They contain many beneficial minerals, such as phosphorus, magnesium, and manganese, which help to prevent hypertension and maintain a healthy weight. They are also important for energy metabolism. Both the fiber in chia seeds and the gelling action that takes place when they are mixed with liquids contribute to feeling full and satisfied, thus reducing food cravings between meals. Unlike flaxseeds, chia seeds do not need to be ground in order to obtain their benefits.

3/4 cup canned coconut milk
1 tbsp. chia seeds
3/4 cup almond milk
1 tbsp. cacao powder
2 tsp. unsweetened flaked coconut

1 tsp. virgin coconut oil
1 tsp. protein powder
1/2 ripe banana
1/2 tsp. vanilla extract

Put the coconut milk and the chia seeds in a blender and leave the seeds to soak for 30 minutes at room temperature. Add all the remaining ingredients with a handful of ice. Blend until smooth.

peaches & cream

see variations page 117

Despite the name of this recipe, there is no cream, but the buttermilk and honey make the juice taste very creamy. Peaches are one of the most delicious fruits and are rich in many vital minerals including potassium, fluoride, and iron. Potassium is an important component of cell and body fluids that help regulate heart rate and blood pressure. Fluoride is a component of bones and teeth and is essential for the prevention of dental cavities. Iron is required for red blood cell formation.

3 fresh ripe peaches, pitted
2/3 cup low-fat buttermilk

1/2 large ripe banana
1 tsp. honey

Juice the peaches and transfer the juice to a blender with the buttermilk, banana, and honey. Add a handful of ice. Blend until smooth.

cinnamon rolls in a glass

see variations page 118

Dates offer numerous health benefits along with their great taste. They are full of fiber, which is essential for promoting colon health and ensuring regular bowel movements. The soluble and insoluble fiber in dates also helps to clean out the gastro-intestinal system, allowing the colon to work at greater levels of efficiency. Fiber is also known to boost heart health, and dates are rich in magnesium, which is known for its anti-inflammatory benefits, as well as for being helpful in combating Alzheimer's disease, arthritis and other inflammation-related health problems.

3 dates, pitted
1/2 cup water
2 fuji or gala apples
1/2 cup Greek-style yogurt
1 tsp. rice or pea protein powder

1 tbsp. ground flaxseed
1 tsp. vanilla extract
1/4 tsp. ground cinnamon
1/2 tsp. lucuma powder

Put the dates and water in a small pan over a medium heat and bring to a boil, stirring occasionally, then reduce the heat and simmer gently for about 5 minutes or until a smooth paste forms. Remove from heat and let cool.

Juice the apples and transfer the juice to a blender. Add the cooled date paste, yogurt, protein powder, ground flaxseed, vanilla extract, cinnamon, and lucuma powder with a handful of ice. Blend until smooth.

peach & papaya

see variations page 119

Papayas are an excellent source of vitamin A, which is necessary for maintaining healthy mucus membranes and skin, and essential for good eyesight. Their antioxidant properties help to protect from oxygen-derived free radicals that play a role in aging and many diseases. Eating fruits rich in carotenes, such as papayas, has been known to help protect the body from lung and oral cavity cancers. Papayas are rich in many essential B-complex vitamins such as folic acid, vitamin B-6, riboflavin, and vitamin B-1.

1 fuji or gala apple
1 pear
1 peach, pitted

1/2 papaya, peeled and seeded
1/2-in. (1-cm) piece fresh gingerroot, peeled
2 mint leaves

Juice all the ingredients, then transfer the juice to a blender. Add a handful of ice and blend until smooth.

variations

apple pie delight

see base recipe page 89

apple pie delight with flaxseed
Prepare the basic recipe, adding 2 teaspoons ground flaxseed to the blender with the banana and other ingredients.

apple pie delight with blackberries
Add 1/3 cup blackberries to the blender with the banana and other ingredients.

apple pie delight with lucuma powder
Add 1 teaspoon lucuma powder to the blender with the banana and other ingredients.

dairy-free apple pie delight with raspberries
Omit the yogurt and milk. Substitute 1/2 cup coconut, almond, or rice milk and add 1/3 cup raspberries to the blender with the banana and other ingredients.

chocolate peanut butter after-school reviver

see base recipe page 90

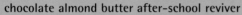

chocolate almond butter after-school reviver
Prepare the basic recipe, omitting the peanut butter and substituting almond butter.

chocolate peanut butter with avocado
Omit the banana and substitute 1/2 avocado, peeled.

gluten-free chocolate peanut butter with flaxseed & protein powder
Omit the wheat germ and substitute 1 teaspoon ground flaxseed and 1 teaspoon protein powder.

dairy-free peanut butter after-school reviver
Omit the milk, substituting coconut, almond, or rice milk.

variations

deconstructed pumpkin pie juice

see base recipe page 93

deconstructed pumpkin pie with walnuts
Prepare the basic recipe, adding 1/4 cup finely chopped walnuts to the blender with the rest of the ingredients.

deconstructed pumpkin pie with flaxseed & protein powder
Add 1 teaspoon ground flaxseed and 1 teaspoon protein powder to the blender with the rest of the ingredients.

deconstructed pumpkin pie with pineapple
Omit the apple and instead juice 1/4 pineapple with the mango. Continue according to the basic recipe.

deconstructed pumpkin pie with peach & ginger
Prepare the basic recipe, omitting the apple, allspice, and cloves. Juice 2 pitted peaches with the mango, and substitute the allspice and cloves with 1/4 teaspoon ground ginger. Blend as before, transfer to a glass, and top up with a dash of ginger beer.

variations

lemonade zinger

see base recipe page 94

lemonade zinger with black currants
Prepare the basic recipe, juicing 1/4 cup black currants with the apples.

hot lemonade zinger with honey
Prepare the basic recipe. Put the juice into a pan and heat gently. Omit the soda water and stir 1 teaspoon honey into the hot juice.

lemonade zinger with orange & blueberries
Substitute 1/4 cup blueberries for the grapes.

pineapple & lemonade zinger
Prepare the basic recipe, omitting 2 apples and substituting 1/4 pineapple.

variations

black currant & banana

see base recipe page 96

black currant & banana with cacao
Prepare the basic recipe, adding 2 teaspoons cacao powder and 1 teaspoon vanilla extract to the blender with the rest of the ingredients.

black currant & banana with pineapple
Juice 1/4 pineapple with the apples and black currants.

black currant & banana with spinach & peanut butter
Juice 1 cup baby spinach with the apples and black currants. Add 1 tablespoon smooth peanut butter to the blender.

dairy-free black currant & banana with coconut
Omit the yogurt, substituting 4 tablespoons coconut milk and 1 teaspoon virgin coconut oil.

variations

pineapple & chocolate

see base recipe page 97

pineapple with cherries & cacao powder
Prepare the basic recipe, juicing 2/3 cup pitted cherries with the apples and pineapple. Omit the unsweetened cocoa powder and substitute cacao powder.

pineapple & chocolate with beets
Juice 1 small raw beet with the apples and pineapple.

pineapple & chocolate with passion fruit
Scoop out the insides of 2 passion fruits and add to the blender with the rest of the ingredients.

pineapple & chocolate with orange
Juice 1 medium peeled orange with the apples and pineapple.

variations

apple & orange with kiwi & banana

see base recipe page 99

apple & orange with passion fruit & banana
Prepare the basic recipe, omitting the kiwi. Add the insides of 2 passion fruits to the blender with the rest of the ingredients.

apple & orange with cucumber & avocado
Omit the kiwi and banana. Juice 1/4 cucumber with the oranges and apple. Add 1/2 avocado, peeled and pitted, to the blender with the juice, coconut milk, and vanilla.

apple & grapefruit with plums & banana
Omit the orange and kiwi. Juice 1 medium peeled grapefruit and 2 pitted plums with the apple.

apple & beetroot with grapes & banana
Omit the orange and juice 1 small raw beetroot and 1/2 cup grapes with the apple.

carrot cake juicy gem

see base recipe page 100

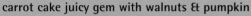

carrot cake juicy gem with walnuts & pumpkin
Prepare the basic recipe, omitting the banana and substituting 1/3 cup pumpkin purée. Also add 1 tablespoon finely chopped walnuts to the blender with the rest of the ingredients.

carrot cake juicy gem with sweet potato
Juice 1/2 small sweet potato, skin on, with the apple, carrots, and pineapple.

carrot cake juicy gem with vanilla
Omit the ginger and allspice and substitute 1 teaspoon vanilla extract. Blend as before.

dairy-free carrot cake with coconut
Omit the buttermilk and oats. Substitute 1/2 cup coconut milk and also add 1 tablespoon unsweetened flaked coconut to the blender with the rest of the ingredients.

variations

chia chocolate coconut protein rush

see base recipe page 103

chia chocolate protein rush with pineapple
Juice 1/4 pineapple and add it to the blender with the rest of the ingredients.

chia chocolate protein rush with orange & carrot
Juice 1 medium peeled orange and 1 small carrot and transfer the juice to a blender with the rest of the ingredients.

chia chocolate protein rush with fresh figs
Juice 2 fresh figs and transfer the juice to a blender with the rest of the ingredients.

chia chocolate protein rush with almonds & plums
Omit the unsweetened flaked coconut. Juice 2 pitted plums and transfer the juice to a blender along with the rest of the ingredients and 1 tablespoon ground almonds.

peaches & cream

see base recipe page 104

peaches & cream with vanilla & lucuma powder
Prepare the basic recipe, adding 1 teaspoon vanilla extract and 1 teaspoon lucuma powder to the blender with the rest of the ingredients. Blend as before.

peaches & cream with raspberries
Add 1/2 cup raspberries to the blender with the rest of the ingredients.

peaches & cream with flaxseed & oats
Add 1 tablespoon ground flaxseed and 1 tablespoon quick-cooking rolled oats to the blender with the rest of the ingredients.

dairy-free peaches & cream with coconut
Omit the buttermilk and substitute 2/3 cup coconut milk. Add 2 tablespoons unsweetened flaked coconut to the blender with the rest of the ingredients.

variations

cinnamon rolls in a glass

see base recipe page 106

cinnamon rolls in a glass with pineapple
Prepare the basic recipe, juicing 1/4 pineapple with the apples.

cinnamon rolls in a glass with carrot
Juice 1 large carrot with the apples.

cinnamon rolls in a glass with figs
Juice 2 figs with the apples.

dairy-free cinnamon rolls in a glass with macadamia nuts
Omit the yogurt and protein powder. Substitute 1/2 cup almond milk and add 1 tablespoon finely chopped macadamia nuts to the blender with the rest of the ingredients.

variations

peach & papaya

see base recipe page 107

peach & papaya with spinach
Prepare the basic recipe, adding 1 cup baby spinach to the juicer with the rest of the ingredients.

peach & papaya with prunes
Add 1/4 cup canned prunes, pitted and well drained, to the blender with the rest of the ingredients.

peach & papaya with carrot & orange
Omit the pear and mint. Juice 1 small carrot and 1 small peeled orange with the apple.

peach & papaya with pineapple
Omit the pear and mint. Juice 1/4 pineapple with the apple.

all fruit

If you are not in the mood for veggies, or you feel

like a juice that is simple and fruity, this chapter

provides plenty of recipes for juices made from

a variety of fruits, with no vegetables in sight.

banana berry special

see variations page 141

Eating berries on a regular basis can improve or prevent metabolic syndrome, which is a medical term for a combination of diabetes, high blood pressure, and obesity. Having all three of the berries in this juice is particularly good for your health. Berries are rich in antioxidants that protect cells in the heart and help lower blood pressure. Blueberries contain a substance that can activate fat-burning genes in fat cells to help with weight loss — with loss from the tummy in particular.

2 fuji or gala apples
1 orange, peeled
1 ripe banana

1/2 cup strawberries, hulled
1/4 cup blueberries
1/3 cup raspberries

Juice the apples and orange. Transfer the juice to a blender and add the banana, strawberries, blueberries, and raspberries with a handful of ice. Blend until smooth.

apple, pear & plum

see variations page 142

Plums contain the minerals potassium, fluoride, and iron, which are necessary for red blood cell formation, and this promotes heart health by helping to regulate blood pressure and heart rate. Vitamin A in plums is essential for healthy eyes and good vision, and the different vitamin B compounds such as niacin, vitamin B-6, and phenolic acid break down and metabolise carbohydrates, proteins, and fat molecules.

2 fuji or gala apples
1 pear
2 plums, pitted

Juice the apples, pear, and plums and serve over ice.

peach, pear & pineapple

see variations page 143

This simple cocktail of fruits is very appealing. Peaches, which can be juiced or blended, are not only full of goodness, but they can also aid weight loss—including lots of fresh, ripe, juicy fruit in your diet is a great way to help control your hunger and lose weight. Peaches contain natural fruit sugars, so they do not raise your blood sugar or insulin levels like processed sugars do. The sweetness of peaches will also help to control cravings for sugary snacks.

2 fresh ripe peaches, pitted
2 pears
1/4 medium pineapple
1 tbsp. ground flaxseed

Juice the peaches, pears and pineapple. Transfer the juice to a blender, add the flaxseed and a handful of ice. Blend until smooth.

strawberry, grape & orange

see variations page 144

Peel the oranges before juicing, but leave the pith on because it contains bioflavonoids, substances that are not required for life but that may improve health. An orange provides a large proportion of the vitamin C that you need for one day. Because of their high vitamin C content, oranges are often credited with boosting the immune system.

2 medium oranges, peeled
10 red grapes
1 3/4 cups strawberries, hulled

Juice the oranges and grapes. Transfer the juice to a blender with the strawberries and a handful of ice. Blend until smooth.

calming goji berry & banana with lavender

see variations page 145

Lavender is not just a fragrant flower, it is also an edible herb that you can use as a remedy for restlessness, insomnia, nervousness, and depression. The oil that lavender contains seems to have sedating effects and might also relax certain muscles of the body. This herb is most often used as an oil, but the flowers can also be crushed and added to muffins, cookies, or drinks such as tea or juices. However, it should be used sparingly as the flavor can be overpowering.

1 cup coconut water
3 tbsp. goji berries
1 frozen banana, sliced into 4 pieces
1/2 cup frozen blueberries
1 tsp. crushed dried lavender flowers

Put the coconut water and goji berries in a blender and leave to soak for 30 minutes. Add the remaining ingredients, except the lavender flowers, with a handful of ice. Blend until smooth. If the fruits in this juice are not frozen, blend with a handful of ice. Sprinkle with the crushed flowers to serve.

red currant & peach

see variations page 146

All berries, including red currants, are packed with nutrients that are particularly beneficial for skin. Red currants in particular are rich in vitamin B-complex and vitamin C, which is a powerful antioxidant that fights — and could even reverse — free radical damage in skin cells. These vitamins help with skin cell regeneration and promote healing from harmful UV ray damage. Berries are also rich in iron, which is essential for the formation of red blood cells.

1 fuji or gala apple
1/3 cup red currants
2 peaches, pitted

1/3 cup blueberries
1/2 cup blackberries
1 tbsp. honey (optional)

Juice the apple, red currants, peaches, blueberries, and blackberries. Transfer the juice to a blender with a handful of ice. Blend until smooth. Sweeten with honey, if desired.

acai apricot & mango

see variations page 147

Some research claims that acai berries are high in an antioxidant that is associated with lowering cholesterol levels in the blood stream, and also in plant sterols, which have been shown to improve blood circulation, helping to prevent blood clots.

2/3 cup pure acai berry juice
4 ripe apricots, pitted and quartered
1/2 mango, peeled, pitted, and cubed

Put all the ingredients in a blender with a handful of ice. Blend until smooth.

orange, strawberry & papaya

see variations page 148

Deliciously sweet with musky undertones and a soft, butter-like consistency, it is no surprise that Christopher Colombus reputedly called the papaya the "fruit of the angels." Once considered quite exotic, they are now found in grocery stores and supermarkets throughout the year. Papayas are low in calories, contain no cholesterol, and are a rich source of phyto-nutrients, minerals, and vitamins.

1 large orange, peeled
1/2 papaya, peeled, seeded, and cubed
1/2 lime, peeled
1/4 medium pineapple

1 1/2 cups strawberries, hulled
1 tbsp. ground flaxseed
1/2 tsp. vanilla extract
1/2 tsp. maca powder

Juice the orange, papaya, lime, and pineapple. Transfer the juice to a blender with the strawberries, ground flaxseed, vanilla extract, maca powder, and a handful of ice. Blend until smooth.

apple, pineapple & cherry berry

see variations page 149

People who suffer from arthritis have reported that drinking pineapple juice alleviates the pain they suffer due to this debilitating disease. Pineapple juice contains bromelain, which appears to have anti-inflammatory properties. It works by neutralizing fluids, to ensure they are not too acidic, and it also helps to regulate the secretions in the pancreas to aid digestion. Bromelain also has protein-digesting activity so it can help to keep the digestive tract healthy.

1 fuji or gala apple
1 peach, pitted
1/4 medium pineapple

2/3 cup pitted cherries
1/2 cup raspberries
3/4 cup strawberries, hulled

Juice the apple, peach, pineapple, and cherries, then transfer the juice to a blender with the raspberries and strawberries. Add a handful of ice. Blend until smooth.

fizzy pineapple, mango, orange & lime

see variations page 150

Limes are anti-carcinogenic. They contain limonoid compounds, which have been shown to prevent cancers of the colon, stomach, and blood. Though the exact way they do this is unknown, scientists have noticed that antioxidant limonoids also can cause cancer cells to die. They stay active in the bloodstream for a comparatively long time, mopping up more free radicals than green tea or dark chocolate.

1/2 medium pineapple
2 medium oranges, peeled
1/2 lime, peeled

1/4 mango, peeled and pitted
4 tbsp. soda water

Juice the pineapple, oranges, lime, and mango. Transfer the juice to a glass with a little ice and top up with the soda water.

peaches & plums with apricots

see variations page 151

Apricots belong to the same family of plants as the garden rose! They taste great and offer a variety of health benefits. Low in calories, they contain lots of vitamin A, a powerful antioxidant that can protect against age-related macular degeneration and may help to promote healthy vision. Apricots are a good source of beta-carotene, and studies have shown that people who eat a diet rich in beta-carotene have a lower risk of some cancers and also heart disease.

2 fresh ripe peaches, pitted and chopped
2 plums, pitted
1/4 medium pineapple
2 fresh ripe apricots, pitted and quartered

4 tbsp. coconut water
1/4 tsp. stevia (optional)
a little grated lemon zest

Juice the peaches, plums, and pineapple. Transfer the juice to a blender. Add the apricots and coconut water with a handful of ice. Blend until smooth. Sweeten if desired with a little stevia and sprinkle with a little grated lemon zest to serve.

variations

banana berry special

see base recipe page 121

banana berry special with spinach
Prepare the basic recipe, juicing 1 cup baby spinach with the apples and orange.

banana berry special with beet
Juice 1 small raw beet with the apples and orange.

banana berry special with plums
Juice 2 pitted plums with the apples and orange.

banana berry special with cherries
Omit the orange. Juice 1 1/4 cups pitted cherries with the apples, and blend as before.

variations

apple, pear & plum

see base recipe page 122

apple, pear & plum with red currants
Prepare the basic recipe, juicing 1/4 cup red currants with the apple, pear, and plums. Transfer the juice to a blender, add 4 tablespoons plain yogurt and a handful of ice. Blend until smooth.

apple, pear & plum with kiwi fruit and alfalfa
Juice 2 peeled kiwi fruit and 1 cup alfalfa sprouts with the apple, pear, and plums.

apple, pear & plum with figs
Juice 2 figs with the rest of the ingredients.

apple, pear & plum with mango
Prepare the basic recipe. Transfer the juice to a blender, add 1/2 mango, peeled and pitted, and a handful of ice. Blend until smooth.

peach, pear & pineapple

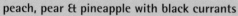

see base recipe page 125

peach, pear & pineapple with black currants
Prepare the basic recipe, juicing 1/3 cup black currants with the peach, pears, and pineapple.

peach, pear & pineapple with banana
Prepare the basic recipe. Transfer the juice to a blender, add the flaxseed, 1/2 ripe banana, 2 tablespoons plain yogurt, and a handful of ice. Blend as before.

peach, pear & pineapple with papaya
Prepare the basic recipe. Transfer the juice to a blender, add the flaxseed, 1/2 peeled and seeded papaya, 1 tablespoon quick-cooking oats, and a handful of ice. Blend until smooth.

peach, pear & pineapple with orange
Prepare the basic recipe, adding 1 medium peeled orange to the juicer with the rest of the ingredients. Transfer the juice to a blender, add the flaxseed and a handful of ice and blend as before.

variations

strawberry, grape & orange

see base recipe page 126

strawberry, grape & orange with cranberries
Prepare the basic recipe, juicing 1/2 cup cranberries with the oranges and grapes.

strawberry, grape & grapefruit
Substitute 1 medium peeled pink grapefruit for the orange.

strawberry, grape & lime with banana
Juice 1 lime, peeled, with the oranges and grapes. Add 1/2 ripe banana and 2 tablespoons plain yogurt to the blender with the rest of the ingredients.

strawberry, grape & orange with cherries & maca
Juice 1/2 cup pitted cherries with the oranges and grapes. Blend as before, adding 1/2 teaspoon maca powder to the blender with the rest of the ingredients.

variations

calming goji berry & banana with lavender

see base recipe page 129

calming goji berry & banana with lavender & yogurt
Prepare the basic recipe, omitting the coconut water and substituting it with whole milk.
Add 2 tablespoons plain yogurt to the blender with the rest of the ingredients.

calming goji berry & banana with lavender & coconut
Omit the coconut water. Substitute coconut milk, and add 2 tablespoons unsweetened flaked
coconut to the blender with the rest of the ingredients.

calming goji berry & banana with raspberries & chocolate
Omit the coconut water and blueberries. Substitute whole milk and raspberries, and add
1 tablespoon unsweetened cocoa powder to the blender with the rest of the ingredients.

calming goji berry & banana with lavender & blackberries
Omit the blueberries, substituting blackberries.

variations

red currant & peach

see base recipe page 130

red currant & peach with figs
Prepare the basic recipe, juicing 2 figs with the rest of the ingredients.

red currant & peach with plums
Juice 2 pitted plums with the rest of the ingredients.

red currant & peach with pineapple
Omit the apple and substitute 1/4 medium pineapple.

red currant & peach with apricots & yogurt
Juice 2 pitted apricots with the rest of the ingredients. Add 2 tablespoons natural yogurt to the blender with the juice.

acai apricot & mango

see base recipe page 133

acai apricot & mango with cherries & black currant
Juice 4 pitted apricots, 1/2 cup pitted cherries and 3 tablespoons black currants. Transfer the juice to a blender with the acai berry juice, mango, and ice, and blend as before.

apricot, prune, mango & peach
Omit the acai juice and substitute prune juice. Juice 2 pitted peaches and add the juice to the blender with the rest of the ingredients.

cranberry, cherry, mango & blueberry
Omit the acai juice and apricots. Juice 2/3 cup cranberries, 1/2 cup pitted cherries and 1/4 cup blueberries. Add the juice to the blender with the mango and ice, and blend as before.

acai apricot & mango with blackberry & flaxseed
Add 1/2 cup blackberries and 1 tablespoon ground flaxseed to the blender with the rest of the ingredients.

orange, strawberry & papaya

see base recipe page 134

orange, strawberry & avocado
Prepare the basic recipe, adding 1/2 peeled and pitted avocado to the blender with the rest of the ingredients.

orange, strawberry & dates
Put 3 dates and 1/2 cup water in a small pan over a medium heat, and bring to a boil, stirring occasionally. Reduce the heat and simmer gently for 5 minutes, or until a smooth paste forms. Remove from the heat and let cool. Juice the orange, lime, and pineapple and add to the blender with the date paste and the rest of the ingredients. Blend as before.

orange & lemon with strawberry & banana
Omit the papaya and lime, substituting lemon for the lime. Add 1 ripe banana to the blender with the rest of the ingredients.

orange & grapefruit, strawberry & figs
Omit the papaya and lime, substituting 1 pink grapefruit for the lime and adding 2 figs to the juicer with the oranges and pineapple.

apple, pineapple & cherry berry

see base recipe page 137

apple, pineapple & cherry berry with spirulina
Prepare the basic recipe, adding 1 teaspoon spirulina to the blender with the
rest of the ingredients.

pear, pineapple & cherry berry
Omit the apple and substitute 2 pears. Add 1 teaspoon maca powder to the blender
with the rest of the ingredients.

apple, pineapple & cherry berry with plums
Juice 2 pitted plums with the apple, peach, pineapple, and cherries.

apple, pineapple & cherry berry with blackberries
Omit the strawberries, substituting 1/2 cup blackberries.

fizzy pineapple, mango, orange & lime

see base recipe page 138

fizzy pineapple, mango, lemon & lime
Prepare the basic recipe. Omit the orange and add 1 peeled lemon to the juicer with the pineapple, lime, and mango.

fizzy pineapple, mango, orange & ginger
Juice 1/2-in. (1-cm) piece fresh gingerroot, peeled, with the pineapple, oranges, lime, and mango. Substitute ginger beer for the soda water.

fizzy pineapple, papaya, orange & grapefruit
Omit the mango and lime. Instead juice 1/2 papaya, peeled and seeded, and 1 peeled medium pink grapefruit with the pineapple and oranges.

fizzy pineapple, mango, lemon & plums
Omit the lime and soda water. Add 2 pitted plums to the juicer with the pineapple and oranges. Transfer the juice to a blender, add the mango, 2 tablespoons yogurt, and a handful of ice. Blend until smooth.

peaches & plums with apricots

see base recipe page 140

peaches & plums with apricots & kumquats
Prepare the basic recipe, juicing 4 kumquats with the peaches, pineapple, and plums.

peaches & plums with kiwis & yogurt
Prepare the basic recipe, omitting the coconut water. Juice 2 peeled kiwis with the peaches, plums, and pineapple. Transfer the juice to a blender, add 5 tablespoons yogurt and a handful of ice. Blend until smooth.

peaches & plums with apricots & coconut
Omit the coconut water and substitute coconut milk. Add 1 tablespoon unsweetened flaked coconut and 1 teaspoon virgin coconut oil to the blender with the apricots and ice.

peaches & plums with apricots & alfalfa sprouts
Add 1 cup alfalfa sprouts to the blender with the juice, apricots, coconut water, and ice. To grow your own alfalfa spouts, spread a double layer of paper towels on a baking sheet and dampen with a little water. Sprinkle with alfalfa sprout seeds, cover loosely with plastic wrap and leave for a few days to sprout. Use within two days.

green detox juices

Made with various green fruits and vegetables, with the occasional bright color thrown in for variation, the juices in this chapter will cleanse and detox your body. For a maximum of three days, try one for breakfast and another two or three during the day, then have a healthy meal in the evening. You will feel great!

green apple martini

see variations page 173

Research has shown that, with its abundance of vitamins and minerals, the kiwi fruit provides a wide range of nutritional benefits. Consuming just two kiwi fruits each day may significantly lower the risk of blood clots and reduce the amount of fats in blood, therefore helping to protect against heart disease. The kiwi fruit contains vitamin C, which will not only help the body to absorb the iron contained in the spinach in this juice, but it also helps to heal wounds and boost the immune system.

1 granny smith apple
2-in. (5-cm) slice of cucumber
2/3 cup green grapes

1/2 cup baby spinach
1 kiwi fruit, peeled

Juice the apple, cucumber, grapes, spinach, and kiwi fruit. Transfer the juice to a glass with 2–3 ice cubes, shake or stir, and serve immediately.

spinach & kale green juice

see variations page 174

Kale is a cruciferous vegetable, like cabbage and broccoli, and has exceptional nutrient richness in the form of antioxidant, anti-inflammatory, and anti-cancer properties. Without sufficient intake of antioxidants, both oxygen metabolism and the body's ability to fight inflammation can become compromised, which can cause the risk of developing cancer. It has been shown that kale has an amazing ability to raise blood levels of the nutrients that are necessary to fight chronic health problems.

1 granny smith apple
1 cup baby spinach
1 cup kale

1 stalk of celery
1/4 cucumber
1/2 lemon, peeled

Put the apple in the funnel of the juicer and pack the spinach and kale on top. Add the celery, cucumber, and lemon. Pour over ice to serve.

apple & lettuce with barley grass

see variations page 175

Barley grass is popular in detox juices because it has a wide range of health benefits. It is richer in individual vitamins and enzymes than many other cereal grasses and is said to be easier on the digestive system than wheat grass. It is sprouted from barley seeds and is best eaten by juicing the grass sprouts at three to seven days old to produce a powerful, fresh green juice. You can also buy it in powder form, which is very easy to include in juices.

1 granny smith apple
1 1/2 cups chopped romaine lettuce
1/4 medium pineapple
1/4 cucumber

1 stalk of celery
1/4 lemon, peeled
1/4 mango, peeled, pitted, and cubed
1 tsp. barley grass powder

Juice the apple, lettuce, pineapple, cucumber, celery, and lemon. Transfer the juice to a blender, add the mango, barley grass powder, and a handful of ice. Blend until smooth.

Thai coconut green juice

see variations page 176

This delicate-tasting juice contains lots of electrolytes and minerals. Naturally refreshing, coconut water has a sweet, nutty taste, fewer calories than coconut milk, and less sugar than soda and fruit juice. It is naturally fat-free and cholesterol-free, it has lots of potassium and is super hydrating. Depending on the size and age of the coconut, you should get 1/2–1 cup coconut water from each coconut.

1 young Thai coconut (or 1/2 cup coconut
    water)
2 pears
1 cup kale

large handful of fresh cilantro
1/4 lime, peeled
1/2 lemon grass stalk

Crack open the coconut and empty the liquid into a large glass.

Juice the pears, kale, cilantro, lime, and lemon grass and stir the juice into the coconut water. Add some ice to serve.

broccoli, spinach, green bell pepper & apple

see variations page 177

Red, green, yellow, and orange bell peppers are low in calories and packed with nutrients. They contain vitamins A and C, and several phytochemicals and carotenoids, particularly beta-carotene, which provides a lot of antioxidant and anti-inflammatory benefits. The capsaicin in bell peppers has been shown to reduce bad cholesterol, control diabetes, and bring relief from pain and inflammation. Using bell peppers raw is advantageous because it means they retain most of their flavonoid content, which is a powerful nutrient.

2 granny smith apples
1 3/4 cups chopped broccoli (spears
   and stalks)

2 cups baby spinach
1/2 green bell pepper
1/2 lime, peeled

Juice all the ingredients and pour over ice to serve.

salad leaves, chard, peach, apricot & cilantro

see variations page 178

Cilantro is a herb that you either love or hate. It contains many compounds that are known to have disease-preventing and health-promoting properties. Its leaves and seeds contain many essential volatile oils and it is a good source of minerals such as potassium, calcium, manganese, iron, and magnesium. It is also rich in many vital vitamins, including folic acid, riboflavin, niacin, vitamin A, and vitamin C. Cilantro is one of the richest herbal sources of vitamin K, which has a potential role in building bone mass.

1 fuji or gala apple
3 cups shredded lettuce leaves
2 cups chard
1 pear
1 peach, pitted
1 apricot, pitted
1/2 tomato
1/4 stalk of celery
1-in. (2.5-cm) slice of cucumber

small handful of fresh cilantro
1/2 cup arugula
2 cups watercress
1/4 avocado, peeled
2 tsp. ground flaxseed
1 tsp. maca powder
1 tsp. green superfood powder
1 tsp. protein powder

Juice the apple, lettuce, chard, pear, peach, apricot, tomato, celery, and cucumber. Transfer the juice to a blender and add the cilantro, arugula, watercress, avocado, flaxseed, maca powder, green superfood powder, protein powder, and a handful of ice. Blend until smooth.

kiwi fruit, pear, orange & avocado with spinach

see variations page 179

Kiwi fruits are one of the few foods that are rich in vitamin B-6, which supports the immune system. This vitamin is particularly important for babies developing in the uterus, and for pregnant and breastfeeding women. The folate in kiwi fruits helps to protects against birth defects, heart disease, and cancer.

1 kiwi fruit, peeled
1 orange, peeled
1 pear

1/2 cup baby spinach
4 tbsp. coconut water
1/2 avocado, peeled

Juice the kiwi fruit, orange, pear, and spinach. Transfer the juice to a blender, add the coconut water, avocado, and a handful of ice. Blend until smooth.

broccoli, cucumber, peach & celery

see variations page 180

Lemons have powerful antibacterial properties. Experiments have found that lemon juice destroys the bacteria of many deadly diseases, such as malaria, cholera, diphtheria, and typhoid, and it has been suggested that they can dissolve uric acid and other poisons. They are also great as a liver detoxifier.

2 granny smith apples
1 peach, pitted
1 3/4 cups chopped broccoli (spears and stalks)

2 stalks of celery
1/4 cucumber
1/2 lemon, peeled

Juice all the ingredients and pour over ice to serve.

zingy cabbage & celery root with zucchini & orange

see variations page 181

Celery root is the brown bulbous root of the celery plant. It has a rustic appearance and a lovely nutty flavor, is high in potassium and also a natural diuretic. It can improve digestion and boost your immune system. Celery root was originally used for medicinal purposes to purify the blood, as it is a stimulating tonic and can curb sweet cravings.

1 pear
1 cup chopped celery root, outer parts
    removed
1 1/4 cups chopped Chinese or savoy cabbage
1 cup chopped broccoli (spears and stalks)

1/4 zucchini
1 small carrot
1/2-in. (1-cm) piece fresh gingerroot
1/2 medium orange, peeled
1/4 lime, peeled

Juice all the ingredients and pour over ice to serve.

green apples, pineapple & asparagus

see variations page 182

Asparagus contains a unique carbohydrate called inulin, which remains undigested until it reaches the large intestine, where it helps the body to absorb nutrients in a more efficient manner, cutting the risk of colon cancer. The vitamin K contained in asparagus is good for healthy blood clotting and strengthening the bones.

3 granny smith apples
10 asparagus spears
1 pear

1/4 medium pineapple
1/4 avocado, peeled

Juice the apples, asparagus, pear, and pineapple. Transfer the juice to a blender, add the avocado, and a handful of ice. Blend until smooth.

watercress, cucumber & carrot

see variations page 183

There was a study in the UK that seemed to show that eating watercress on a regular basis has an amazing effect on the appearance of facial skin. According to the study, ten out of eleven volunteers experienced visible improvements to their skin after just four weeks of adding one bag of watercress a day to their diet. One woman even managed to reduce her facial wrinkles by an incredible 39 percent. Generally, there was an improvement in overall appearance, wrinkles, texture, pores, red areas, and brown spots. In fact the results were extremely positive and the majority of women also reported increased energy levels. In the study, the watercress had to be eaten raw, but could be consumed in any way they wanted, so adding it to juices is ideal.

2 granny smith apples
1/4 medium pineapple
1/4 cucumber

1 medium carrot
1/2 lemon, peeled
3 cups watercress

Juice the apples, pineapple, cucumber, carrot, and lemon. Transfer the juice to a blender, add the watercress, and a handful of ice. Blend until smooth.

kiwi fruit, cucumber, spinach & watercress

see variations page 184

Avocados are low in sugar and high in monounsaturated fat, which is considered a good fat, as it reduces levels of bad cholesterol in blood and lowers the risk of diabetes, stroke, and coronary heart disease. Avocados also contain protein and potassium and are rich in vitamins B, C, E, and K. Eating avocados is generally associated with better diet quality and nutrient intake, and it has been found that people who eat avocados are more likely to have a lower body weight, body mass index, and waist measurement.

2 granny smith apples
2 kiwi fruit, peeled
1 cup baby spinach
1/4 medium pineapple
2-in. (5-cm) slice of cucumber

1/4 lime, peeled
1 1/3 cups watercress
1/4 avocado, peeled
1 tsp. green superfood powder

Juice the apples, kiwi fruit, spinach, pineapple, cucumber, and lime. Transfer the juice to a blender, and add the watercress, avocado, superfood powder, and a handful of ice. Blend until smooth.

pear, orange, romaine, carrot & cucumber

see variations page 185

Pears are a rich source of copper, phosphorus, and potassium, and also contain calcium, iron, magnesium, sodium, and sulfur. They have a high pectin content, which makes pears useful in helping to reduce cholesterol levels. They are thought to be a diuretic, and also have a mild laxative effect, so drinking pear juice regularly may help to regulate bowel movements. The high amounts of natural sugars found in pears will provide you with a quick boost of energy when you need one.

3 cups chopped romaine lettuce
2 large carrots
1/4 cucumber
2 oranges, peeled

1 pear
1/4 lime, peeled
1/4 avocado, peeled
1 tsp. green superfood powder

Juice the lettuce, carrots, cucumber, oranges, pear, and lime. Transfer the juice to a blender. Add the avocado, green superfood powder, and a handful of ice. Blend until smooth.

variations

green apple martini

see base recipe page 153

green apple martini with celery
Prepare the basic recipe, omitting the cucumber and substituting 1/2 stalk of celery.

green apple martini with broccoli
Omit the cucumber and juice 1 broccoli stalk with the rest of the ingredients.

green apple martini with lime
Omit the cucumber, substituting 1/2 lime.

green apple martini: retox while you detox
Add 2 tablespoons vodka to the juice.

spinach & kale green juice

see base recipe page 154

spinach & green grapes juice
Prepare the basic recipe, omitting the kale and substituting 1 1/3 cups green grapes.
Transfer the juice to a blender, add 2 tablespoons plain yogurt and a handful of ice
and blend until smooth.

spinach & green bell pepper juice
Omit the kale, substituting 1/2 green bell pepper.

spinach & parsley green juice
Omit the kale, substituting 1 large handful of fresh parsley.

spinach, kale & ginger green juice
Juice 1/2-in. (1-cm) piece fresh gingerroot with the rest of the ingredients.

variations

apple & lettuce with barley grass

see base recipe page 157

apple & lettuce with barley grass & broccoli
Prepare the basic recipe, adding 2 broccoli stalks to the juicer with the rest of
the ingredients.

apple & lettuce with barley grass & spinach
Add 1 cup spinach to the juicer with the rest of the ingredients.

apple & lettuce with barley grass & asparagus
Add 4 asparagus spears to the juicer with the rest of the ingredients.

apple & lettuce with barley grass & parsley
Add a handful of fresh parsley to the juicer with the rest of the ingredients.

Thai coconut green juice

see base recipe page 158

Thai coconut green juice with apple & mint
Prepare the basic recipe, omitting the pears and substituting 2 granny smith apples.
Add 4 mint leaves to the juicer with the rest of the ingredients.

Thai coconut green juice with coconut milk
Omit the coconut water. Prepare the basic juice. Transfer the juice to a blender with
1 cup coconut milk, and a handful of ice. Blend until smooth.

Thai coconut green juice with celery & basil
Omit the cilantro. Add 1 stalk of celery and 6 basil leaves to the juicer with the rest of
the ingredients.

Thai coconut green juice green with green bell pepper
Add 1/2 green bell pepper to the juicer with the rest of the ingredients.

broccoli, spinach, green bell pepper & apple

see base recipe page 159

broccoli, spinach, beet & pear
Prepare the basic recipe, omitting 1 apple and the green bell pepper. Substitute 1 small beet and 2 pears.

broccoli, spinach, grape & carrot
Omit 1 apple and the green bell pepper. Substitute 1 small carrot and 2/3 cup green grapes.

broccoli, spinach, asparagus & apple
Omit the green bell pepper, substituting 6 asparagus spears.

broccoli, spinach, pineapple & apple
Omit 1 apple and substitute 1/4 pineapple. Juice as before. Transfer the juice to a blender, add 2 tablespoons plain yogurt, 1/4 avocado, peeled, and a handful of ice and blend until smooth.

variations

salad leaves, chard, peach, apricot & cilantro

see base recipe page 160

salad leaves, beans, peach, apricot & dandelion
Prepare the basic recipe, omitting the chard and cilantro. Juice 8 string beans and
1 tablespoon dandelion leaves with the apple, salad leaves, pear, peach, apricot, tomato,
celery, and cucumber.

salad leaves, beet, peach, apricot & basil
Omit the chard and cilantro. Juice 1 small beet and 2 tablespoons basil leaves with the
other ingredients.

salad leaves, kiwi, peach, apricot & lime
Omit the chard and cilantro. Juice 1 peeled kiwifruit with the other ingredients.

salad leaves, chard, peach, apricot, watermelon & banana
Prepare the juice, omitting the cilantro, then transfer the juice to a blender, add 1 medium
slice peeled watermelon, 1/2 ripe banana and the rest of the ingredients, omitting the
avocado, and blend as before.

variations

kiwifruit, pear, orange & avocado with spinach

see base recipe page 163

kiwifruit, pear, lemon & avocado with spinach & ginger
Prepare the basic recipe, omitting the orange and substituting 2 peeled lemons. Juice
1-cm (1/2-in) piece fresh gingerroot with the kiwifruit, lemons, pear, and spinach.

kiwifruit, apple, orange & banana with spinach
Omit the avocado, substituting 1 apple and 1/2 ripe banana. Blend as before.

kiwifruit, pear, lime & carrot with parsley
Omit the orange. Juice 1 lime, 1 carrot, and a small handful of fresh parsley with the
kiwifruit, pear, and spinach and blend as before.

kiwifruit, apple, grapefruit & banana with mango
Omit the orange. Juice 1 apple and 1/4 peeled grapefruit with the kiwifruit, pear, and
spinach, and transfer the juice to a blender. Add 1/4 mango, peeled and pitted, with the rest
of the ingredients and blend as before.

broccoli, cucumber, peach & celery

see base recipe page 164

broccoli, cucumber, peach & celery with ginger
Prepare the basic recipe, juicing 1/2-in. (1-cm) piece fresh gingerroot with the rest of the ingredients.

broccoli, beet, peach & pear with lime
Omit the celery, cucumber and lemon. Juice 1 small beet, 1 pear and 1/4 peeled lime with the apples, peach, and broccoli.

broccoli, cucumber, peach & celery with carrot
Juice 1 small carrot with the rest of the ingredients.

broccoli, cucumber, peach & asparagus
Omit the celery. Juice 8 asparagus spears with the apples, peach, broccoli, cucumber, and lemon.

zingy cabbage & celery root with zucchini & orange

see base recipe page 167

zingy cabbage & celery root with zucchini & figs
Juice 2 figs with the rest of the ingredients.

zingy cabbage & celery root with zucchini & grapefruit
Omit the orange and substitute 1/4 peeled grapefruit.

zingy cabbage & celery root with zucchini & kiwifruit
Omit the carrot. Juice 1 peeled kiwifruit with the rest of the ingredients.

zingy cabbage & celery root with zucchini & beet
Omit the carrot. Juice 1 small beet with the rest of the ingredients.

variations

green apples, pineapple & asparagus

see base recipe page 168

green apples, pineapple & cherries
Prepare the basic recipe, omitting the asparagus. Substitute 1/2 cup pitted cherries.

green apples, pineapple & kiwi fruit
Omit the asparagus. Juice 1 peeled kiwi fruit with the apples, pear, and pineapple and blend as before.

green apples, pineapple & summer fruits
Make the juice, omitting the asparagus. Transfer the juice to a blender, omit the avocado and add 1 1/2 cups frozen summer fruits and 2 tablespoons plain yogurt. Blend until smooth.

green apples, pineapple & strawberry
Omit the asparagus. Transfer the juice to a blender, add 1 1/2 cups hulled strawberries with the avocado and ice and blend until smooth.

watercress, cucumber & carrot

see base recipe page 169

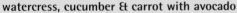

watercress, cucumber & carrot with avocado
Prepare the basic recipe. Add 1/4 avocado, peeled, to the blender with the rest of the ingredients.

watercress, cucumber & carrot with broccoli
Add 1-in. (2.5-cm) piece of broccoli stalk to the juicer with the rest of the ingredients.

watercress, cucumber & carrot with kiwi fruit
Add 1 peeled kiwi fruit to the juicer with the apples, pineapple, cucumber, carrot, and lemon.

watercress, cucumber & carrot with banana
Add 1/2 ripe banana and 2 tablespoons plain yogurt to the blender with the rest of the ingredients.

kiwifruit, cucumber, spinach & watercress

see base recipe page 171

kiwifruit, cucumber, spinach & watercress with broccoli
Prepare the basic recipe, adding 2 broccoli stalks to the juicer with the apples, kiwifruit, spinach, pineapple, cucumber, and lime.

kiwifruit, cucumber, spinach & watercress with cilantro
Add a small handful of fresh cilantro to the blender with the rest of the ingredients.

kiwifruit, cucumber, spinach & watercress with peach
Juice 1 pitted peach with the apples, kiwifruit, spinach, cucumber, and lime.

kiwifruit, cucumber, spinach & watercress with oats & peanut butter
Add 1 tablespoon quick-cooking oats and 1 tablespoon peanut butter to the blender with the rest of the ingredients.

pear, orange, romaine, carrot & cucumber

see base recipe page 172

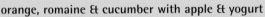

orange, romaine & cucumber with apple & yogurt
Prepare the juice, omitting the carrots, 1 orange and the pear. Instead, juice 2 apples with the romaine lettuce, cucumber, 1 orange, and lime. Transfer the juice to a blender. Omit the avocado and add the green superfood powder, 1/2 ripe banana, 5 tablespoons plain yogurt, and a handful of ice. Blend until smooth.

orange, romaine, carrot & cucumber with cilantro
Prepare the basic recipe, juicing a handful of fresh cilantro with the other ingredients.

orange, romaine, carrot & melon
Omit the cucumber when making the juice. Add 1 medium slice peeled melon to the blender with the rest of the ingredients.

orange, romaine, carrot & apricot
Omit the cucumber, substituting 2 pitted apricots.

juice blends

There is no reason why juice mixes should not also look like milkshakes. Even if they include vegetables, the addition of dairy products—or coconut or rice milk—can make a big difference to the appearance and appeal of a detoxifying health drink.

spinach, apple, strawberry & banana

see variations page 206

Strawberries provide a great shot of folic acid, manganese, and potassium. They also contain significant amounts of phytonutrients and flavonoids. They have been used throughout history in a medicinal context to help with digestive ailments, teeth whitening, and also skin irritations. They contain both fiber and fructose, which may help to regulate blood sugar levels by slowing digestion, and the fiber is thought to have a satiating effect, making you feel more satisfied after eating.

1 cup baby spinach
1 fuji or gala apple
1 1/2 cups strawberries, hulled

1 ripe banana
5 tbsp. plain yogurt

Juice the spinach and apple. Transfer the juice to a blender, add the strawberries, banana, yogurt, and a handful of ice. Blend until smooth.

Carly's superfood smoothie

see variations page 207

One of the most powerful benefits of guarana is its energising effects. It has a similar chemical structure to that of caffeine, and the seeds provide even more of a kick. As guarana is released more slowly into the body than caffeine, it provides sustained energy, and the plant directly stimulates the central nervous system, so it may be taken in small doses to fight fatigue and increase activity levels.

1 1/2 cups frozen mixed berries
3 tbsp. quick-cooking oats
2 cups chopped kale

1 cup orange juice
1 tsp. green superfood powder
1/2 tsp. guarana powder

Place all the ingredients in a blender with a handful of ice. Blend until smooth.

boost-your-system juice blend

see variations page 208

Black currants have antibacterial properties and are excellent for urinary tract health. Antioxidant foods are good to include in your diet because they can be effective against cancer and early signs of aging. They help improve memory, strengthen bones and teeth, and increase oxygen supply to the brain, all of which makes the black currant one of the healthiest fruits around.

3/4 cup strawberries, hulled	1/2 cup Greek-style yogurt
1/3 cup blueberries, plus extra to serve	1 tbsp. ground flaxseed
1/3 cup black currants	1 tbsp. maple syrup
1 banana	1 tsp. green superfood powder
1/2 cup coconut water	1/2 tsp. ground cinnamon

Place all the ingredients in a blender with a handful of ice. Blend until smooth. Serve garnished with extra blueberries, if liked.

blackberry, mango & honey

see variations page 209

Blackberries are rich in bioflavonoids and vitamin C. They are low in calories and sodium, and have one of the highest antioxidant levels of all fruits. Antioxidants are well-known for lowering the risk of cancer. They may help to promote the healthy tightening of tissue, which is a great non-surgical procedure to make skin look younger. Prolonged consumption also helps keep the brain alert, having a positive impact on motor and cognitive skills, thereby maintaining clarity of thought and a good memory.

1 cup blackberries
1/4 mango, peeled and pitted
1/4 ripe banana

1 tsp. honey
1 cup plain yogurt
1/2 cup coconut water

Place all the ingredients in a blender, add a handful of ice. Blend until smooth.

apricot & almond with psyllium

see variations page 210

Psyllium is native to Iran and India, and traditional medicine typically uses the seeds of the plant. In the West it is usually used as a supplement that is made from the husk. It is a laxative that has also been suggested as a treatment for obesity, diarrhea, colon cancer, irritable bowel syndrome, excess gas, and hemorrhoids. Psyllium is also a well-known ingredient in "bulk laxatives" and should be used with care. It should always be accompanied by plenty of water or other liquid.

2 fuji or gala apples
4 apricots, pitted
1 peach, pitted
1/4 medium pineapple

1/4 cucumber
1/4 lime, peeled
4 tbsp. almond milk
1 tsp. psyllium husk powder

Juice the apples, apricots, peach, pineapple, cucumber, and lime. Transfer the juice to a blender and add the almond milk, psyllium, and a handful of ice. Blend until smooth.

iced coffee, pineapple & banana

see variations page 211

Yogurt is loaded with vitamins, potassium, phosphorous, riboflavin, iodine, zinc, and vitamin B-5. It also contains B-12, which maintains red blood cells and helps to keep the nervous system functioning properly. The probiotics in some yogurts balance the microflora in the gut, which can aid digestion and strengthen the immune system. Yogurt is also high in calcium and the live cultures in yogurt help the body to absorb the calcium.

2 fuji or gala apples
1/4 medium pineapple
1/2 ripe banana

4 tbsp. plain yogurt
1 tsp. maple syrup
1 tsp. instant coffee powder

Juice the apples and pineapple. Transfer the juice to a blender, add the banana, yogurt, maple syrup, coffee powder, and a handful of ice. Blend until smooth.

peanut butter, banana & spinach with rice milk

see variations page 212

Rice milk is made from boiled rice, brown rice syrup, and brown rice starch. It is popular with people who are lactose intolerant, and also with vegetarians and vegans, because it contains no animal products or by-products. It contains more carbohydrates than cow's milk, but it is lower in calories and, unlike cow's milk, it does not contain lactose or cholesterol, which makes it heart-healthy.

1 cup rice milk
2 tbsp. peanut butter
2 tbsp. ground flaxseed

2 cups baby spinach
1 ripe banana

Place all the ingredients in a blender, and a handful of ice. Blend until smooth.

blueberry & avocado bananamaca

see variations page 213

Blueberries are one of the richest sources of proanthocyanidins, which reduce levels of free radicals. They are packed with vitamin C, E, riboflavin, niacin, and folate. Some research suggests that blueberries may improve motor skills and memory, and possibly reverse some age-related memory loss and motor skill decline.

1 1/2 cups blueberries
2 fuji or gala apples
1 pear

1/2 ripe banana
1/4 avocado, peeled
1 tsp. maca powder

Juice the blueberries, apple, and pear. Transfer the juice to a blender, add the banana, avocado, maca powder, and a handful of ice. Blend until smooth.

pomegranate, blackberry, fig & coconut

see variations page 214

Pomegranate seeds are rich in phytochemicals, which are beneficial substances found in minute quantities in plant foods. The types of phytochemicals found in pomegranate seeds are known as polyphenols (such as tannins, and quercetin) and anthocyanins, all of which may offer both heart health and anti-cancer benefits. As powerful antioxidants, polyphenols may improve healthy cell survival, cause the death of cancer cells and help prevent the growth of tumors. Anthocyanins not only have anti-inflammatory properties, but also antiviral and antimicrobial qualities as well.

2 pomegranates	6 ripe figs
2 cups blackberries	1/3 cup coconut milk

First remove the seeds from the pomegranates. To do so, hold a pomegranate on its side and cut a thin slice from the top and bottom. Put the pomegranate on its base and cut four shallow slits through the skin, from the top to the bottom. Peel off the skin and discard it, leaving the pith and the seeds behind. Now peel the seeds away from the pith and discard the pith. Repeat with the second pomegranate.

Pack the pomegranate seeds from both pomegranates into the funnel of a juicer. Pack the blackberries tightly on top and juice on the slow speed. Juice the figs. Transfer the juice to a blender, add the coconut milk, and a handful of ice. Blend until smooth.

pumpkin, plum & orange juice blend

see variations page 215

Plums—like strawberries and other red berries—contain an antioxidant that can protect against cancer and cell damage. This fruit is low in calories and has a low glycemic index, so eating plums can help to control blood sugar levels and reduce the risk of type-2 diabetes. Plums also contain sorbitol and isatin, which help to regulate the digestive system so that the body has the ability to digest different foods. It has also been reported that extracts from plums can destroy aggressive breast cancer cells without harming the surrounding tissue.

2 plums, pitted
1 large orange, peeled
2 tbsp. pumpkin purée
2 tbsp. plain yogurt
1 tsp. maple syrup

1/2 tsp. vanilla extract
1/4 tsp. ground cinnamon
pinch of ground ginger
pinch of ground nutmeg

Juice the plums and orange and transfer the juice to a blender. Add the pumpkin purée, yogurt, maple syrup, vanilla extract, cinnamon, ginger, nutmeg, and a handful of ice and blend until smooth.

apple & raspberry with flaxseed & almond butter

see variations page 216

Raspberries contain a phytonutrient called rheosmin, also known as raspberry ketone, which has the ability to increase not only enzyme activity, but oxygen consumption, and heat production in certain types of fat cells. This puts fat metabolism into overdrive, thus decreasing the risk of obesity, as well as fatty liver disease. Raspberry ketone has also been known to decrease the activity of a fat-digesting enzyme that is released by the pancreas.

2 fuji or gala apples
1 cup raspberries
1/2 ripe banana

1/3 cup almond milk
2 tsp. almond butter
2 tsp. ground flaxseed

Juice the apples and transfer the juice to a blender. Add the raspberries, banana, almond milk, almond butter, flaxseed, and a handful of ice. Blend until smooth.

fig & banana with almond milk & vanilla

see variations page 217

Figs are recommended for the prebiotics they contain because they can help support the pre-existing good bacteria in the gut, improving digestive efficiency. They are also an excellent source of calcium, which is good for bone density, and their high potassium level may counteract the urinary excretion of calcium caused by high-salt diets. This goes on to help preserve calcium in bones and reduce the risk of osteoporosis.

4 fresh figs
1 fuji or gala apple
1 ripe banana

1 cup almond milk
1 tsp. vanilla extract

Juice the figs and apple, then transfer the juice to a blender. Add the banana, almond milk, vanilla extract, and a handful of ice. Blend until smooth.

variations

spinach, apple, strawberry & banana

see base recipe page 187

chocolaty spinach, apple, strawberry & banana
Prepare the basic recipe, adding 2 teaspoons cacao powder to the blender with the rest of the ingredients.

spinach, pineapple, strawberry & banana
Omit the apple and substitute 1/4 medium pineapple.

spinach, plum, strawberry & banana
Omit the apple and substitute 3 pitted plums. Blend as before.

spinach, apple, strawberry & banana with figs
Juice 2 figs with the spinach and apple.

variations

Carly's superfood smoothie

see base recipe page 188

Carly's superfood smoothie with almonds
Prepare the basic recipe, omitting 2 tablespoons quick-cooking oats and substituting
1 tablespoon ground almonds. Add 1 tablespoon almond butter to the blender with the
rest of the ingredients.

Carly's superfood smoothie with maca powder
Omit the guarana. Substitute 1 teaspoon maca powder and add 2 tablespoons vanilla
yogurt to the blender with the rest of the ingredients.

Carly's superfood smoothie with peanut butter
Omit the orange juice. Substitute rice milk and add 1 tablespoon smooth peanut butter
to the blender with the rest of the ingredients.

Carly's superfood smoothie with coconut
Omit the orange juice. Substitute coconut milk and add 1 tablespoon unsweetened flaked
coconut to the blender with the rest of the ingredients.

variations

boost-your-system juice blend

see base recipe page 191

boost-your-system blend with spirulina and almonds
Prepare the basic recipe, omitting the coconut water and substituting almond milk. Add 1 tablespoon ground almonds and 1 teaspoon spirulina to the blender with the rest of the ingredients.

boost-your-system blend with avocado
Add 1/4 avocado, peeled, to the blender with the rest of the ingredients.

boost-your-system blend with raspberries
Add 1/2 cup raspberries to the blender with the rest of the ingredients.

dairy-free boost-your-system blend
Omit the coconut water and yogurt. Substitute 1 cup canned coconut milk.

blackberry, mango & honey

see base recipe page 192

blackberry, apricot, mango & maple syrup
Prepare the basic recipe, omitting 1/2 cup blackberries and substituting 3 chopped apricots. Substitute 2 teaspoons maple syrup for the honey and blend as before.

blackberry, raspberry, mango & honey with maca powder
Omit 1/2 cup blackberries and substitute 1/2 cup raspberries. Add 1 teaspoon maca powder to the rest of the ingredients in the blender.

blackberry, peach, mango & honey
Omit 1/2 cup blackberries and substitute 2 chopped peaches.

dairy-free blackberry, cherry, mango & almond
Omit 1/2 cup blackberries, the yogurt and the coconut water. Substitute 1/2 cup pitted cherries and 1 cup almond milk.

apricot & almond with psyllium

see base recipe page 195

apricot, almond & spinach with psyllium

Prepare the basic recipe, juicing 1/2 cup baby spinach with the apples, apricots, pineapple, cucumber, and lime.

chocolate, apricot & almond with psyllium

Add 2 teaspoons unsweetened cocoa powder to the blender with the rest of the ingredients.

apricot & almond with psyllium & oats

Add 1 tablespoon quick-cooking oats to the blender with the rest of the ingredients.

apricot, kiwifruit & almond with psyllium

Juice 1 peeled kiwifruit with the apples, apricots, peach, pineapple, cucumber, and lime.

iced coffee, pineapple & banana blend

see base recipe page 196

iced cacao, pineapple & banana blend with flaxseed
Prepare the basic recipe, substituting 2 teaspoons cacao for the instant coffee powder, and adding 1 tablespoon ground flaxseed to the blender with the rest of the ingredients.

iced mocha pineapple & banana blend with mango
Add 1 teaspoon unsweetened cocoa powder and 1/4 mango, peeled, pitted, and cubed, to the blender with the rest of the ingredients.

iced coffee, pineapple & banana blend with peach
Juice 2 pitted fresh peaches with the apples and pineapple.

iced dairy-free coffee, pineapple & banana blend with apricot
Juice 2 pitted apricots with the apples and pineapple. Transfer the juice to the blender, omit the yogurt and substitute 4 tablespoons coconut milk.

peanut butter, banana & spinach with rice milk

see base recipe page 198

almond butter, banana & spinach with almond milk
Prepare the basic recipe, omitting the peanut butter and rice milk. Substitute almond butter and almond milk, and add 1 tablespoon ground almonds to the rest of the ingredients in the blender.

peanut butter, banana & spinach with yogurt & avocado
Omit the rice milk. Substitute 1/2 cup plain yogurt and 4 tablespoons coconut water, and add 1/4 avocado, peeled, to the blender with the rest of the ingredients.

peanut butter, mango & spinach with rice milk & protein powder
Omit the banana. Substitute 1 small mango, peeled and pitted, and add 1 teaspoon protein powder to the blender with the rest of the ingredients.

peanut butter, banana & spinach with chocolate milk
Omit the rice milk and substitute whole milk. Add 2 teaspoons unsweetened cocoa powder to the blender with the rest of the ingredients.

blueberry & avocado bananamaca

see base recipe page 199

blueberry, cherry & avocado bananamaca
Prepare the basic recipe, juicing 1/2 cup pitted cherries with the blueberries, apple, and pear.

blueberry, fig & avocado bananamaca
Juice 2 figs with the blueberries, apple, and pear.

blueberry, peach & avocado bananamaca
Juice 1 pitted peach with the blueberries, apple, and pear.

blueberry, kumquat & avocado bananamaca
Juice 4 kumquats with the blueberries, apple, and pear.

pomegranate, blackberry, fig & coconut

see base recipe page 201

pomegranate, blueberry, fig & coconut
Prepare the basic recipe, omitting the blackberries and substituting blueberries.

pomegranate, blackberry, fig & apricot
Juice 2 pitted apricots with the pomegranate seeds, blackberries, and figs.

pomegranate, peaches, fig & coconut
Juice 2 pitted peaches with the pomegranate seeds, blackberries, and figs.

pomegranate, blackberry, fig & yogurt
Omit the coconut milk. Substitute 1/2 cup plain yogurt.

pumpkin, plum & orange juice blend

see base recipe page 202

pumpkin, plum & orange juice blend with basil
Prepare the basic recipe, juicing 1 tablespoon basil leaves with the plums and orange.

pumpkin, plum & orange juice blend with strawberry & flaxseed
Add 1 1/2 cups hulled strawberries and 1 tablespoon ground flaxseed to the blender with the rest of the ingredients.

pumpkin, plum & orange juice blend with figs
Juice 2 figs with the plums and orange.

pumpkin, plum & orange juice blend with banana
Add 1/2 ripe banana to the blender with the rest of the ingredients.

apple & raspberry with flaxseed & almond butter

see base recipe page 204

pear & raspberry with passion fruit & almond butter
Prepare the juice, omitting 1 apple and substituting 1 pear. Cut 1 passion fruit in half, scoop out the insides, and add the seeds and pulp to the blender with the rest of the ingredients.

apple & raspberry with kiwi fruit & almond butter
Peel 1 kiwi fruit and juice it with the apples.

apple & cherry with protein powder & peanut butter
Juice 1 cup pitted cherries with the apples. Transfer the juice to the blender, omit the flaxseed and raspberries and add 1 teaspoon protein powder to the blender with the rest of the ingredients.

apple & raspberry with fig & almond butter
Juice 2 fresh figs with the apples.

variations

fig & banana with almond milk & vanilla

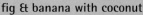

see base recipe page 205

fig & banana with coconut
Prepare the basic recipe, omitting the almond milk and substituting coconut milk. Add
1 tablespoon unsweetened flaked coconut to the blender with the rest of the ingredients.

fig & banana with Greek-style yogurt
Omit the almond milk and substitute 1 cup Greek-style yogurt.

fig & banana with chocolate
Add 2 teaspoons cacao powder to the blender with the rest of the ingredients.

fig & banana with avocado
Add 1/4 avocado, peeled, to the blender with the rest of the ingredients.

red detox juices

The recipes in this chapter are made with mostly red fruits and vegetables, which are known to provide an amazing number of antioxidants that have a fantastic impact on mood and vitality, and look particularly appetizing because of their attractive and vibrant colors.

beet & carrot with parsley & echinacea

see variations page 239

Echinacea has long been used as a remedy for the common cold and other upper respiratory infections. Take it to combat the symptoms of an infection — research suggests that echinacea may modestly reduce cold symptoms, but it is not clear whether it helps to prevent colds from developing. You can also use it against other infections such as the flu, urinary tract infections, yeast infections, septicemia, gum disease, and tonsillitis, to name just a few.

2 small beets
2 medium carrots
1 fuji or gala apple
1/3 cup black currants

2 tbsp. fresh parsley
1/4 lemon, peeled
1 tsp. echinacea

Juice all the ingredients and pour over ice to serve.

red cabbage & ginger
with lemon

see variations page 240

Red cabbage will give you glowing skin and a powerful immune system. Ancient healers declared it to be moon food, because it grew in the moonlight, and we now know that its power comes from the high sulfur and vitamin C content. It is very low in calories and commonly thought of as "brain food" as it is full of vitamin K and anthocyanins that help with mental function and concentration. These nutrients also help to prevent nerve damage, improving the body's defence against Alzheimer's disease and dementia.

2 cups chopped red cabbage
1 small beet
3 fuji or gala apples

1 lemon, peeled
1/2-in. (1-cm) piece fresh gingerroot

Juice all the ingredients and pour over ice to serve.

red currant, avocado & strawberry with lucuma

see variations page 241

Lucuma powder is made from the subtropical fruit of the lucuma tree, native to Peru, Chile, and Ecuador, and is usually sold in powder form. It is said to have a taste that is somewhere between maple syrup and pumpkin, and is quite often used as a flavoring. It also delivers an abundance of health benefits, as it is a rich source of antioxidants, fiber, carbohydrates, vitamins, and minerals, all of which are necessary for optimum health.

2/3 cup red currants
1/4 small beet
2 fuji or gala apples
1/2 stalk of celery
1/2 lemon, peeled

1/4 avocado, peeled
1 1/2 cups strawberries, hulled
1/2 cup coconut water
1 tsp. lucuma powder

Juice the red currants, beet, apples, celery, and lemon. Put the juice in a blender with the avocado, strawberries, coconut water, lucuma powder, and a handful of ice. Blend until smooth.

tomato & romaine with red bell pepper, plum & chile

see variations page 242

There are many benefits of eating tomatoes, but the biggest is the fact that they contain the antioxidant lycopene, which helps to mop up damaging free radicals in the body that can harm the cells. Lycopene may help to ward against prostate cancer, breast cancer, stomach cancer, and age-related macular degeneration. It can boost the skin's ability to protect itself against UV rays, and some studies suggest that lycopene may also help to reduce bad cholesterol.

1 fuji or gala apple
1 tomato
2 red plums, pitted
1 small carrot
1 cup baby spinach
1/2 red bell pepper, seeded

1 cup chopped romaine lettuce
1 stalk of celery
1/4 small beet
1/4 fresh jalapeño pepper
1 tbsp. chopped chives

Juice all the ingredients and pour over ice to serve.

raspberry, red currants & grapes with wheat germ

see variations page 243

Wheat germ is the most vitamin- and mineral-rich part of the wheat kernel. This is because it is the part that will nourish the new wheat plant, which is why it has so many wonderful nutrients. It is full of B vitamins that are important for a healthy heart and to keep our brains supplied with good mood chemicals. It also contains lots of fiber, which is necessary for good blood sugar balance, cholesterol control, intestinal health, and detoxing.

2 fuji or gala apples
1 1/3 cups red grapes
1/2 cup chopped red cabbage
1/3 cup red currants

1/4 lime, peeled
2 cups raspberries
1/4 mango, peeled, pitted, and cubed
2 tsp. wheat germ

Juice the apples, grapes, red cabbage, red currants, and lime. Transfer the juice to a blender, add the raspberries, mango, wheat germ, and a handful of ice. Blend until smooth.

red bell pepper & carrot with melon & cayenne pepper

see variations page 244

Cayenne pepper has in the past been used for a variety of ailments, including heartburn, delirium, gout, dyspepsia, flatulence, sore throat, tonsillitis, and scarlet fever. It is a well-known digestive aid as it can stimulate the digestive tract, increasing the flow of enzyme production and gastric juices. This helps the body to metabolize food and toxins, relieving intestinal gas and keeping the bowel working efficiently. Research has suggested that participants in a study who took cayenne pepper for breakfast were found to have less appetite, leading to less calories consumed throughout the day.

1 medium carrot
1/2 red bell pepper, seeded
1/2 cup chopped red cabbage
1 fuji or gala apple

1/8 medium pineapple
2 cups watermelon, peeled and cubed
pinch of cayenne pepper

Juice the carrot, red bell pepper, red cabbage, apple, and pineapple. Transfer the juice to a blender. Add the melon, cayenne pepper, and a handful of ice. Blend until smooth.

beet, apple & blackberry macalucuma

see variations page 245

Lucuma powder contains fourteen essential trace elements, including a considerable amount of potassium, sodium, calcium, magnesium, and phosphorus. Phosphorus is important for bone and protein formation, digestion, and hormone balance. Lucuma also contains carbohydrates, fiber, protein, and a small amount of fat, and has calcium to keep bones and teeth strong. Blackberries can be juiced or blended, so if you prefer, omit them from the juicer and blend them with the powders and ice instead.

2 small beets
2 fuji or gala apples
2 red plums, pitted

1 cup blackberries
1 tsp. maca powder
1 tsp. lucuma powder

Juice the beets, apples, plums, and blackberries. Transfer the juice to a blender, add the maca powder, lucuma powder, and a handful of ice. Blend until smooth.

peach, cranberry, carrot & orange

see variations page 246

Peaches are high in antioxidants—in particular, one called chlorogenic acid, which is known to protect the body from cancer and other chronic diseases. This antioxidant is also helpful for reducing inflammation in the body, which is good for those suffering from arthritis, and it helps to slow the aging process. Consuming peaches is an excellent way of cleansing toxins from the colon, kidneys, stomach, and liver. They are rich in potassium, which reduces kidney related diseases and the chance of developing ulcers.

2 peaches, pitted
1 1/4 cups fresh cranberries
2 medium carrots

2 large oranges, peeled
1/2-in. (1-cm) piece fresh gingerroot

Juice all the ingredients and pour over ice to serve.

red cabbage & blueberry with sesame

see variations page 247

Sesame seeds are rich in monounsaturated fatty acids, which help to lower bad cholesterol and increase good cholesterol. They are also a valuable source of dietary proteins with quality amino acids that are essential for growth, especially in children. They are considered a nutrient powerhouse, rich also in calcium, iron, manganese, zinc, magnesium, selenium, and copper. Many of these minerals have a vital role to play in bone mineralisation, red blood cell production, enzyme synthesis, hormone production, and regulation of cardiac and skeletal muscle action.

2 cups chopped red cabbage
1/4 cucumber
1 fuji or gala apple

1 1/3 cups red grapes
1 1/2 cups blueberries
1 tsp. sesame seeds

Juice the red cabbage, cucumber, apple, grapes, and 1 cup of the blueberries. Transfer the juice to a blender, add the remaining blueberries, the sesame seeds, and a handful of ice. Blend until smooth.

watermelon, cherry & strawberry

see variations page 248

Watermelons have an alkaline-forming effect in the body when fully ripe, and eating lots of alkaline-forming foods can help to reduce the risk of developing disease and illness caused by a high-acid diet (from eating meat, eggs, and dairy products). The vitamin C content is also very high. The enzymes involved in forming collagen, the main component of wound healing, cannot function without vitamin C, so if you ever suffer from a slow-healing wound, up your intake of fruit rich in vitamin C.

1 fuji or gala apple
1 small beet
1 tomato
8 basil leaves

1/2 cup pitted cherries
2 cups watermelon, peeled and cubed
1/2 cup strawberries, hulled

Juice the apple, beet, tomato, and basil leaves. Transfer the juice to a blender, add the cherries, watermelon, strawberries, and a handful of ice. Blend until smooth.

spicy tomato

see variations page 249

Worcestershire sauce is packed with vitamins that may help many health conditions. It has been suggested that Worcestershire sauce has the ability to increase efficiency of the immune system as it contains vitamin B-6 foods such as molasses, garlic, cloves, and chilli pepper extract. Vitamin B-6 helps to build red blood cells and assists in keeping the nervous system healthy, and may even keep your mood positive, and your skin healthy. The vitamin E that is also present in Worcestershire sauce contributes to a strong immune system, and the antioxidants offer protection against aging as they improve the appearance of the skin and help keep hair loss under control.

4 ripe tomatoes
2 fuji or gala apples
1 stalk of celery
1/2 red bell pepper, seeded
1 tsp. Worcestershire sauce

1/2 tsp. onion powder
1/2 tsp. garlic powder
1/4 tsp. freshly ground black pepper
pinch of cayenne pepper

Juice the tomatoes, apples, celery, and red bell pepper. Transfer the juice to a blender, add the Worcestershire sauce, onion powder, garlic powder, freshly ground black pepper, cayenne pepper, and a handful of ice. Blend until smooth.

pomegranate & cherry plum

see variations page 250

Raspberries are rich in B-complex vitamins and also in vitamin K. These vitamins help the body metabolise carbohydrates, protein and fats. They also contain valuable amounts of minerals such as potassium, manganese, copper, iron and magnesium. Potassium is an important component of cell and body fluids and helps to control heart rate and blood pressure.

seeds from 1/2 pomegranate
4 red plums, pitted
1 cup pitted cherries

1/4 medium pineapple
1/4 cup raspberries

First remove the seeds from the pomegranate. To do this, cut a thin slice from the top and bottom. Put the pomegranate on its base and cut 4 shallow slits through the skin, from the top to the bottom. Peel off the skin and discard it, leaving the pith and the seeds behind. Now peel the seeds away from the pith and discard the pith. Put half the seeds in the funnel of the juicer (you can use the remaining pomegranate seeds in other recipes — store them in the refrigerator in an airtight container for up to one week).

Juice the pomegranate seeds, plums, cherries, and pineapple. Transfer the juice to a blender, add the raspberries, and a handful of ice. Blend until smooth.

eggplant, red currant & orange

see variations page 251

Eggplants contain certain essential phytonutrients that improve blood circulation and are thought to nourish the brain. Eggplants are also instrumental in contributing to heart health, as research studies show that they can reduce bad cholesterol and are high in bioflavonoids, which are known to control high blood pressure and relieve stress. They also contain chlorogenic acid, a plant compound that is known for its high antioxidant activity, shielding the cells from oxidation (which is a harmful chemical process that damages the cells and contributes to disease).

1 fuji or gala apple
1 medium orange, peeled
1/2 cup cubed eggplant
3 tbsp. red currants

1/3 cup blackberries
1/8 medium pineapple
2-in. (5-cm) slice of cucumber

Juice all the ingredients, then transfer the juice to a blender. Add a handful of ice. Blend until smooth.

variations

beet & carrot with parsley & echinacea

see base recipe page 219

beet & carrot with basil & chile
Prepare the basic recipe, omitting the parsley. Juice 1/2 green chile and 8 basil leaves with the rest of the ingredients.

beet & carrot with lime & cilantro
Omit the parsley and lemon. Juice 1/4 lime and a small handful of fresh cilantro with the rest of the ingredients.

beet & carrot with orange & chives
Omit the parsley and lemon. Juice 1 small peeled orange and 2 tablespoons chopped chives with the rest of the ingredients.

beet & carrot with red bell pepper & oregano
Omit the parsley. Juice 1/2 red bell pepper and 2 tablespoons fresh oregano leaves with the rest of the ingredients.

variations

red cabbage & ginger with lemon

see base recipe page 220

red cabbage & ginger with orange
Prepare the basic recipe, omitting the lemon and substituting 1 small peeled orange.

red cabbage & ginger with grapefruit
Omit the lemon, substituting 1/4 peeled pink grapefruit.

red cabbage & ginger with lemon & cranberry
Omit 1 cup red cabbage and juice 1/2 cup fresh cranberries with the rest of the ingredients.

red cabbage & ginger with lemon & plum
Omit 1 cup red cabbage and juice 3 red pitted plums with the rest of the ingredients.

red currant, avocado & strawberry with lucuma

see base recipe page 223

red currant, avocado & strawberry with basil
Prepare the basic recipe, juicing 8 basil leaves with the red currants, beet, apples, celery, and lemon.

red currant, avocado & strawberry with peach & maca powder
Juice 1 pitted peach with the red currants, beet, apples, celery, and lemon. Omit the lucuma powder from the blender and substitute 1 teaspoon maca powder.

red currant, avocado & raspberry with lucuma
Omit the strawberries, substituting raspberries.

red currant, avocado & strawberry with tomato
Juice 1 tomato with the red currants, beet, apples, celery, and lemon.

tomato & romaine with red bell pepper, plum & chile

see base recipe page 224

tomato & romaine with red bell pepper, cranberry, plum & chile
Prepare the basic recipe, omitting the carrot and celery. Juice 1/2 cup fresh cranberries with the rest of the ingredients and transfer the juice to a blender with a handful of ice.

tomato & chard with red bell pepper, plum & parsley
Omit the romaine lettuce and chives. Substitute 1 cup chard and 1 tablespoon parsley.

tomato & red cabbage with red bell pepper, plum & cilantro
Omit the romaine lettuce and chives. Substitute 1/2 cup chopped red cabbage and 1 tablespoon fresh cilantro.

tomato & arugula with red bell pepper, plum & ginger
Omit the romaine lettuce. Juice 1/2-in. (1-cm) piece fresh gingerroot with the rest of the ingredients and transfer the juice to a blender. Add 1/2 cup arugula, and a handful of ice. Blend until smooth.

raspberry, red currants & grapes with wheat germ

see base recipe page 225

strawberry, red currants & grapes with wheat germ
Prepare the basic recipe, omitting the raspberries and substituting strawberries.

raspberry, red currants & grapes with red bell pepper
Juice 1/2 red bell pepper with the apples, grapes, red cabbage, red currants, and lime.

raspberry, red currants & grapes with tamarind
Add 1/4 teaspoon tamarind paste to the blender with the rest of the ingredients.

raspberry, red currants & grapes with banana & lucuma powder
Omit the mango and wheat germ. Add 1/2 ripe banana and 1 teaspoon lucuma powder to the blender with the rest of the ingredients.

red bell pepper & carrot with melon & cayenne pepper

see base recipe page 226

red bell pepper & carrot with strawberry & cayenne pepper
Prepare the basic recipe, omitting the melon. Add 3/4 cup hulled strawberries to the blender with the rest of the ingredients.

red bell pepper & carrot with tomato & cayenne pepper
Omit the melon and juice 1 tomato with the carrot, red bell pepper, red cabbage, apple, and pineapple.

red bell pepper & carrot with red currant & cayenne pepper
Prepare the basic recipe, omitting the melon, and juice 1/3 cup red currants with the carrot, red bell pepper, red cabbage, apple, and pineapple. Then add 1 teaspoon maple syrup to the blender with the juice, cayenne pepper, and ice.

red bell pepper & carrot with cranberries & cayenne pepper
Omit the melon. Juice 2/3 cup fresh cranberries with the carrot, red bell pepper, red cabbage, apple, and pineapple.

variations

beet, apple & blackberry macalucuma

see base recipe page 229

beet, banana & blackberry with banana & protein powder
Prepare the basic recipe. Omit the maca and lucuma powders and add 1/2 ripe banana and 1 teaspoon protein powder to the blender with the juice and ice.

beet, mango & blackberry with flaxseed
Omit the maca powder, and add 1/2 ripe mango, peeled, pitted, and cubed, and 2 teaspoons ground flaxseed to the blender with the rest of the ingredients.

beet, papaya & blackberry with guarana
Omit the lucuma powder and add 1/2 ripe papaya, peeled, seeded, and cubed, and 1/2 teaspoon guarana to the blender with the rest of the ingredients.

beet, apple & blueberry with chia seeds
Omit the blackberries and maca and lucuma powders. Juice 1 1/2 cups blueberries with the beet, apples, and plums and transfer the juice to the blender. Add 1 tablespoon chia seeds and leave to soak for 30 minutes. Add a handful of ice. Blend until smooth.

peach, cranberry, carrot & orange

see base recipe page 230

peach, cranberry, carrot & orange with radishes
Prepare the basic recipe, adding 3 radishes to the juicer with the rest of the ingredients.

peach, cranberry, carrot & orange with cherries
Juice 1 cup pitted cherries with the rest of the ingredients.

peach, cranberry, carrot & orange with tomato & basil
Add 1 tomato and 8 basil leaves to the juicer with the rest of the ingredients.

peach, cranberry, pineapple & orange with rhubarb
Omit the carrot. Juice 1/4 medium pineapple and 1/2 cup diced rhubarb with the rest of the ingredients.

variations

red cabbage & blueberry with sesame

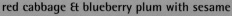

see base recipe page 233

red cabbage & blueberry plum with sesame
Prepare the basic recipe, juicing 2 pitted plums with the red cabbage, cucumber, apple, grapes, and blueberries.

red cabbage & blueberry cherry with sesame
Omit the 1 cup of blueberries in the blender. Substitute 1 cup pitted cherries.

red cabbage & blueberry with watermelon & sesame
Omit the 1 cup of blueberries in the blender. Substitute 1/2 cup watermelon, peeled and cubed.

red cabbage & blueberry with raspberries & almond
Omit the 1 cup of blueberries and the sesame seeds in the blender. Substitute 1/2 cup raspberries and 2 tablespoons ground almonds.

variations

watermelon, cherry & strawberry

see base recipe page 234

watermelon, cherry & strawberry with yogurt
Prepare the juice and transfer it to the blender. Add 2 tablespoons plain yogurt to the blender with the rest of the ingredients.

watermelon, cherry & strawberry with banana
Add 1/2 ripe banana to the blender with the rest of the ingredients.

watermelon, cherry & cranberry with pineapple
Prepare the juice, omitting the beet. Juice 1/2 cup fresh cranberries and 1/4 medium pineapple with the apple, tomato, and basil.

watermelon, cherry & plum with star anise
Juice 2 pitted plums with the apple, beet, tomato, and basil. Add 1 star anise pod to the blender with the rest of the ingredients.

spicy tomato

see base recipe page 235

spicy tomato & orange
Juice 1 small orange with the tomatoes, apples, celery, and red bell pepper.

spicy tomato & ginger
Juice 1/2-in. (1-cm) piece fresh gingerroot with the tomatoes, apples, celery, and red bell pepper.

spicy tomato & cilantro
Juice a small handful of fresh cilantro with the tomatoes, apples, celery, and red bell pepper.

spicy tomato & chives
Juice 2 tablespoons chopped chives with the tomatoes, apples, celery, and red bell pepper.

pomegranate & cherry plum

see base recipe page 236

pomegranate & cherry plum with rhubarb
Prepare the basic recipe, juicing 1/2 cup chopped rhubarb with the pomegranate seeds, plums, cherries, and pineapple.

pomegranate & cherry plum with blackberries
Omit 2 of the plums. Juice 1/2 cup blackberries with the pomegranate seeds, 2 plums, cherries, and pineapple.

pomegranate & cherry plum with red grapes
Omit 2 of the plums. Juice 2/3 cup red grapes with the pomegranate seeds, 2 plums, cherries, and pineapple.

pomegranate & cherry plum with red currants
Omit 2 of the plums. Juice 1/3 cup red currants with the pomegranate seeds, plums, cherries, and pineapple.

eggplant, red currant & orange

see base recipe page 238

eggplant, red currant & orange with figs
Prepare the basic recipe, juicing 2 figs with the rest of the ingredients.

eggplant, red currant & orange with beet
Juice 1/2 small beet with the rest of the ingredients.

eggplant, red currant & orange with yogurt
Add 4 tablespoons plain yogurt to the blender with the juice and ice.

eggplant, red currant & orange with peach
Juice 2 pitted fresh peaches with the rest of the ingredients.

exotic
fruit juices

Exotic fruits such as guava and papaya contribute

not only goodness and a richness of flavor, but

also color and texture. The drinks in this chapter

combine a selection of these flavors and textures

in a variety of delicious blends. The colors speak for

themselves!

pineapple, mango, banana & strawberry

see variations page 272

Eating bananas on a regular basis may help overcome depression due to the high levels of tryptophan, which is converted into serotonin, the good-mood brain neurotransmitter. Used extensively around the world by elite sportsmen and sportswomen, bananas are extremely useful in protecting against muscle cramps and helping to sustain blood sugar levels. They counteract calcium loss and build strong bones. Bananas can also act as a prebiotic, stimulating the growth of friendly bacteria in the bowel, producing digestive enzymes that help the body to absorb nutrients from the foods we eat.

1 mango, peeled and pitted
1 fuji or gala apple
1 pear
1/4 medium pineapple

1 ripe banana
3/4 cup strawberries, hulled
1 tsp. maca powder

Juice the mango, apple, pear, and pineapple. Transfer the juice to a blender, add the banana, strawberries, maca powder, and a handful of ice. Blend until smooth.

tropic of mango & kiwi fruit

see variations page 273

Coconut oil is classed as a superfood because of its unique combination of fatty acids that can have profound positive effects on health. In the past it was thought that, because coconut oil contains saturated fat, it should be avoided. In fact, coconut oil does not contain the average saturated fats such as those found in cheese or steak. It contains medium chain triglycerides, which are fatty acids that are metabolized differently. They go straight to the liver from the digestive tract, where they are used as a quick source of energy, or turned into ketone bodies, which can have a therapeutic effect on brain disorders like epilepsy or Alzheimer's disease.

1 small orange, peeled
1 kiwi fruit, peeled
1/2 mango, peeled, pitted, and cubed
1/4 medium pineapple

1/2 cup blackberries
1/3 cup coconut water
1 tsp. virgin coconut oil

Juice the orange, kiwi fruit, mango, and pineapple. Transfer the juice to a blender and add the blackberries, coconut water, coconut oil, and a handful of ice. Blend until smooth.

passion fruit, tofu and blackcurrant

see variations page 274

Originating in China, tofu—or bean curd—is a popular food derived from soya. It is made by curdling fresh soya milk, pressing it into a solid block and then cooling it, just as dairy cheese is made. It is a good source of protein and contains all eight essential amino acids. Tofu is an excellent source of iron and calcium, and the minerals manganese, selenium, and phosphorous. Tofu is a very filling, satisfying food, but always buy organic, which is made from non-genetically-modified (Non-GMO) soya beans. If you find you have a reaction to soya, use lactose-free cream cheese as a substitute.

1 fuji or gala apple
1/3 cup blackcurrants
1/4 medium pineapple
1/4 cucumber
1/4 lime, peeled

2 passion fruits
1/4 cup silken tofu (or lactose-free cream cheese)
2 tbsp. plain yogurt
1 tsp. vanilla extract

Juice the apple, blackcurrants, pineapple, cucumber, and lime. Transfer the juice to a blender. Halve the passion fruits, scoop out the insides and add to the blender with the tofu, yogurt, vanilla extract, and a handful of ice. Blend until smooth.

pineapple, spinach, mango & lime

see variations page 275

Studies have shown that flavoring a high-carbohydrate food with cinnamon can help to lessen its impact on blood sugar levels, as cinnamon slows the rate at which the stomach empties after meals, reducing the rise in blood sugar after eating. One study showed that less than half a teaspoon of cinnamon each day reduced blood sugar levels in people with type-2 diabetes, and even consuming a small amount each day produced a drop in blood sugar levels.

2 pears
1/4 medium pineapple
1 cup baby spinach
1/2 mango, peeled, pitted, and cubed

1/4 lime, peeled
3 tbsp. pumpkin purée
1/4 tsp. ground cinnamon
1/4 tsp. ground nutmeg

Juice the pears, pineapple, spinach, mango, and lime. Transfer the juice to a blender, add the pumpkin purée, cinnamon, nutmeg, and a handful of ice. Blend until smooth.

pomegranate, papaya, guava & pineapple

see variations page 276

Not only do pomegranates have an amazing color, but drinking pomegranate juice could help to keep Alzheimer's disease at bay as the antioxidants found in this exotic fruit may help reduce the build-up of harmful proteins that can cause the disease. One study found that people who drank pomegranate juice had lower levels of cortisol, which is also known as the stress hormone.

seeds from 1/2 pomegranate
2 guavas
1 fuji or gala apple
1/2 papaya, peeled and seeded

1/4 small pineapple
1/3 cup blackcurrants
1/4 mango, peeled and pitted
1/4-in. (5-mm) piece fresh gingerroot

First remove the seeds from the pomegranate. To do this, cut a thin slice from the top and bottom. Put the pomegranate on its base and cut 4 shallow slits through the skin, from the top to the bottom. Peel off the skin and discard it, leaving the pith and the seeds behind. Now peel the seeds away from the pith and discard the pith. Put half the seeds in the funnel of the juicer (you can use the remaining seeds in other recipes — store them in the refrigerator in an airtight container for up to 1 week).

Juice the pomegranate seeds, guavas, apple, papaya, pineapple, blackcurrants, mango, and ginger, then transfer the juice to a blender with a handful of ice. Blend until smooth.

peach, papaya & pear

see variations page 277

Ginger has a unique warm and zingy flavor. Historically, ginger is recorded to have been highly effective in alleviating symptoms of gastrointestinal distress, and we now know this is because it possesses numerous therapeutic properties, including antioxidants and anti-inflammatories. Ginger is very safe and effective in treating the symptoms of nausea and vomiting during pregnancy — even the most severe form — and it can help to alleviate motion sickness and sea sickness.

2 fresh peaches, pitted
1 pear
1 medium orange, peeled
1 fuji or gala apple

1/2 papaya, peeled and seeded
1/2-in. (1-cm) piece fresh gingerroot
3 mint leaves

Juice the peaches, pear, orange, apple, papaya, ginger, and mint. Transfer the juice to a blender. Add a handful of ice. Blend until smooth.

fig, guava, grape & blueberry

see variations page 278

Guava is a tropical fruit that is highly nutritious. It is soft when ripe, with a sweet musky aroma and creamy texture. Each fruit contains numerous tiny, semi-hard edible seeds. Guavas are a super fruit—they are low in calories and fats, but contain several vital vitamins, minerals and antioxidant polyphenolic and flavonoid compounds that play a pivotal role in the prevention of cancers.

4 small figs
2 fuji or gala apples
2 guavas

2/3 cup red grapes
1/3 cup blueberries
1/2 cup Greek-style yogurt

Juice the figs, apples, guavas, and grapes. Transfer the juice to a blender, add the blueberries, yogurt, and a handful of ice. Blend until smooth.

melon, tamarind, tahini & avocado

see variations page 279

Tamarind, also known as the "Indian date," is packed with nutrients. It is a good source of antioxidants, fiber and potassium, which are all effective in treating inflammations of the heart arteries or walls, caused by heart disease. It is also effective at preventing cardiovascular diseases, as its anti-cholesterol properties help destroy plaque that may accumulate in the arteries surrounding the heart. The high vitamin C content in tamarind makes it excellent for the body's natural defence and immune system.

2 fuji or gala apples
1/4 medium pineapple
1/4 small melon, peeled

1/4 avocado, peeled
2 tsp. tahini
1/4 tsp. tamarind paste

Juice the apples and pineapple. Transfer the juice to a blender, add the melon, avocado, tahini, tamarind paste, and a handful of ice. Blend until smooth.

passion plum, orange & mango

see variations page 280

The edible seeds of the passion fruit are an integral part of the fruit and are somewhat difficult to separate from the pulpy insides. Passion fruit should not be placed in the juicer. Instead, cut them in half, scoop out the insides into the blender and discard the skin. The seeds deliver an abundance of nutritional and health benefits, ranging from antioxidant protection to the maintenance of healthy cardiovascular and intestinal systems. They are rich in polyphenolic compounds (that can protect against the development of cancers, cardiovascular diseases, diabetes, osteoporosis, and neurodegenrative diseases) and they deliver lots of dietary fiber and magnesium.

1 medium orange, peeled
2 plums, pitted
2 passion fruit

1/2 ripe banana
1/4 mango, peeled, pitted, and cubed

Juice the orange and plums. Transfer the juice to a blender. Cut the passion fruit in half, scoop out the insides and add to the blender with the banana, mango, and a handful of ice. Blend until smooth.

spicy orange & pineapple with pumpkin

see variations page 281

Chiles contain a substance called capsaicin, which gives them their characteristic pungency. Their heat can be mild or intense, but the hotter the chile pepper, the more capsaicin it contains. Red chile peppers, such as cayenne, have been shown to reduce bad cholesterol, and capsaicin not only has been shown to reduce pain, but its peppery heat also stimulates secretions that help to clear mucus from a stuffy nose or congested lungs. Added to that, chiles can help prevent stomach ulcers by killing bacteria you may have ingested while, at the same time, stimulating the cells lining the stomach to secrete protective buffering juices.

2 large oranges, peeled
1/4 medium pineapple
1 kiwi fruit, peeled
1/2 lemon, peeled

1/4-in. (5-mm) piece fresh gingerroot
4 tbsp. pumpkin purée
large pinch of chile powder

Juice the oranges, pineapple, kiwi fruit, lemon, and ginger, then transfer the juice to a blender. Add the pumpkin purée, chile powder, and a handful of ice. Blend until smooth.

custard apple, mango & orange

see variations page 282

Custard apples can help to control blood pressure because they contain vitamin A, which also keeps skin and hair healthy. They are excellent for the digestive system, as the copper content helps to combat constipation. The magnesium in custard apples helps to equalize the water balance in the body, removing acids from the joints and reducing the symptoms of rheumatism and arthritis. And if you are tired, the potassium present in custard apples will help to fight muscle weakness. If you cannot obtain custard apples, there is a variation using apple, pear and yogurt (see page 282).

2 custard apples
1 mango, peeled, pitted, and cubed

1 large orange, peeled
1/4 medium pineapple

Juice the custard apples, mango, orange, and pineapple. Transfer the juice to a blender, add a handful of ice. Blend until smooth.

guava, pineapple & star fruit

see variations page 283

Star fruit is a juicy tropical fruit grown in Thailand, throughout Southeast Asia, Australia, South America, and also in Hawaii and Florida. This delicious fruit is a good source of vitamin C, and is full of antioxidants and flavonoids. One word of warning though—if you have kidney problems, you should avoid eating star fruit. Consult your physician if necessary.

2 star fruit
2 small guavas
1 fuji or gala apple
1/4 medium pineapple

1/4 lime, peeled
1/4 avocado, peeled
pinch of ground cinnamon, to serve

Juice the star fruit, guavas, apple, pineapple, and lime. Transfer the juice to a blender, add the avocado, and a handful of ice. Blend until smooth. Sprinkle with a little ground cinnamon to serve.

variations

pineapple, mango, banana & strawberry

see base recipe page 253

pineapple, mango, banana & strawberry with spinach
Prepare the basic recipe, juicing 1/2 cup baby spinach with the mango, apple, pear, and pineapple.

pineapple, mango, banana & strawberry with cucumber
Blend 1/4 cucumber with the mango, apple, pear, and pineapple.

pineapple, mango, banana & strawberry with blackcurrant & yogurt
Juice 1/3 cup blackcurrants with the mango, apple, pear, and pineapple. Transfer the juice to the blender, add 2 tablespoons yogurt with the rest of the ingredients and blend as before.

pineapple, mango, banana & strawberry with blackberries
Juice 1/2 cup blackberries with the mango, apple, pear, and pineapple.

tropic of mango & kiwifruit

see base recipe page 254

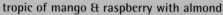

tropic of mango & raspberry with almond
Prepare the basic recipe, omitting the blackberries, and coconut water. Substitute
1/2 cup raspberries and 1/3 cup almond milk.

tropic of mango & kiwi fruit with peaches
Omit the blackberries. Juice 2 pitted peaches with the orange, kiwi fruit, mango, and
pineapple and blend as before.

tropic of mango & kiwifruit with apricots
Omit the blackberries. Juice 2 pitted apricots with the orange, kiwifruit, mango, and
pineapple.

tropic of mango & kiwi with papaya & coconut milk
Omit the blackberries and coconut water and substitute 1/4 papaya, peeled and seeded,
and 1/3 cup coconut milk.

variations

passion fruit, tofu & black currant

see base recipe page 256

passion fruit, tofu & blackcurrant with mango
Prepare the basic recipe, adding 1/4 mango, peeled, pitted, and cubed, to the blender with the rest of the ingredients.

passion fruit, tofu & blackcurrant with watercress
Add 1 1/3 cups watercress to the blender with the rest of the ingredients.

passion fruit, tofu & blackcurrant with kiwi fruit
Juice 1 peeled kiwi fruit with the apple, blackcurrants, pineapple, cucumber and lime.

dairy-free passion fruit, tofu & black currant with apricot & almond
Prepare the basic recipe, omitting the yogurt and vanilla. Juice 2 pitted fresh apricots with the apple, blackcurrants, pineapple, cucumber, and lime. Transfer the juice to the blender. Add 4 tablespoons almond milk, 1 teaspoon almond extract, the tofu, and the ice and blend.

pineapple, spinach, mango & lime

see base recipe page 257

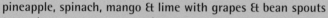

pineapple, spinach, mango & lime with grapes & bean spouts
Juice 2/3 cup red grapes and 1/2 cup bean sprouts with the pears, pineapple, spinach, mango, and lime.

pineapple, spinach, mango & lime with kumquats & vanilla
Prepare the basic recipe, juicing 6 kumquats with the pears, pineapple, spinach, mango, and lime. Add 1 teaspoon vanilla extract to the blender with the rest of the ingredients.

pineapple, spinach, mango & lime with asparagus & wheat grass
Juice 6 asparagus spears with the pears, pineapple, spinach, mango, and lime. Add 1 teaspoon wheat grass powder to the blender with the rest of the ingredients.

pineapple, spinach, mango & lime with blackberries
Prepare the basic recipe. Add 1/2 cup blackberries to the blender with the rest of the ingredients.

variations

pomegranate, papaya, guava & pineapple

see base recipe page 259

pomegranate, papaya, banana & pineapple
Omit the guava and add 1/2 ripe banana to the blender with the rest of the ingredients.

pomegranate, melon, guava & pineapple
Prepare the basic recipe, omitting the papaya and adding 2/3 cup melon, peeled and cubed, to the blender with the rest of the ingredients.

pomegranate, cherry, guava & pineapple
Omit the papaya and add 1 cup pitted cherries to the blender with the rest of the ingredients.

pomegranate, passion fruit, guava & pineapple
Omit the papaya. Cut 1 passion fruit in half and scoop out the insides. Add to the blender with the rest of the ingredients.

variations

peach, papaya & pear

see base recipe page 260

peach, papaya & pear with mango
Juice 1/3 cup mango, peeled and pitted, with the rest of the ingredients.

peach, papaya & pear with melon
Omit the orange. Add 2/3 cup melon, peeled, to the blender with the juice and blend as before.

peach, papaya & pear with banana
Prepare the juice and transfer it to the blender with 1/2 ripe banana and the ice.

peach, papaya & pear with beet
Omit the ginger. Juice 1 small beet with the rest of the ingredients.

fig, guava, grape & blueberry

see base recipe page 262

fig, guava, mango & blueberry
Omit the grapes when making the juice. Add 1/4 mango, peeled, pitted, and cubed, to the blender with the rest of the ingredients.

fig, guava, tomato & coconut water
Omit the figs and grapes when making the juice. Substitute 2 tomatoes. Transfer the juice to a blender. Omit the blueberries and yogurt and add 4 tablespoons coconut water to the blender with the ice.

fig, guava, peach & blackberry
Omit the grapes and juice 2 pitted peaches with the figs, apples and guava. Transfer the juice to a blender. Omit the blueberries and add 1/2 cup blackberries to the blender with the rest of the ingredients.

dairy-free fig, guava, apricot & blueberry
Omit the grapes and juice 2 pitted apricots with the figs, apples, and guava. Transfer the juice to a blender. Omit the yogurt and add 1/2 cup coconut milk to the blender with the rest of the ingredients.

melon, tamarind, tahini & avocado

see base recipe page 263

melon, peach, tamarind, almond butter & passion fruit
Juice 2 pitted peaches with the apples and pineapple. Halve 2 passion fruit, scoop out the insides and add to the blender with the juice, melon, avocado, ice, and 1 teaspoon almond butter. Omit the tahini.

melon & apricot, tamarind, peanut butter & banana
Omit 1 apple and juice 2 pitted apricots with 1 apple and the pineapple. Add 1/2 ripe banana to the blender with the juice, melon, ice, and 1 teaspoon peanut butter, omitting the tahini and avocado.

melon & kiwi, tamarind, tahini & mango
Juice 1 peeled kiwi with the apples and pineapple. Add 1/4 mango, peeled, pitted, and cubed, to the blender with the juice, melon, tahini, tamarind and ice, omitting the avocado.

melon & blackberry, tamarind, cashew butter & yogurt
Add 1/2 cup blackberries and 1/3 cup plain yogurt to the blender with the rest of the ingredients, omitting the tahini and avocado.

passion plum, orange & mango

see base recipe page 265

kiwi fruit, plum, orange & mango
Juice 2 peeled kiwi fruits with the orange and plums. Put the juice in the blender and add the other ingredients, omitting the passion fruit.

passion pear, orange & mango
Omit the plums and substitute 2 pears.

passion pineapple, orange & mango
Omit the plums and substitute 1/4 pineapple.

passion plum, orange & papaya
Omit the mango & substitute 1/4 papaya, peeled and seeded.

spicy orange & pineapple with pumpkin

see base recipe page 266

spicy orange & pineapple with pumpkin & papaya
Add 1/4 papaya, peeled, seeded, and cubed, to the blender with the rest of the ingredients.

spicy orange & pineapple with pumpkin & ugli fruit
Add 1/2 peeled ugli fruit to the blender with the rest of the ingredients.

spicy orange & pineapple with pumpkin & goji berries
Prepare the juice and transfer it to the blender. Add 2 tablespoons goji berries and leave to soak for 30 minutes. Add the rest of the ingredients and blend.

spicy orange & pineapple with pumpkin & mango
Add 1/2 mango, peeled, pitted, and cubed, to the blender with the rest of the ingredients.

variations

custard apple, mango & orange

see base recipe page 269

apple, mango, orange & pear with yogurt

Omit the custard apple. Juice 2 fuji or gala apples and 1 pear with the mango, orange, and pineapple. Add 1 tablespoon plain yogurt to the blender with the juice and ice.

custard apple, mango & orange with ginger beer

Add 1/2 ripe banana to the blender with the rest of the ingredients, and blend as before. Transfer the juice to a glass and top up with a little ginger beer.

custard apple, mango & orange with coconut

Add 4 tablespoons coconut milk and 1 tablespoon unsweetened flaked coconut to the blender with the rest of the ingredients.

custard apple, mango & orange with blackberry & vanilla yogurt

Add 1/2 cup blackberries, 2 tablespoons yogurt, and 1 teaspoon vanilla extract to the blender with the rest of the ingredients.

guava, pineapple & star fruit

see base recipe page 270

guava, pineapple & star fruit with passion fruit
Cut 2 passion fruit in half, scoop out the insides, and add to the blender with the rest of the ingredients.

guava, pineapple & star fruit with blackcurrants & yogurt
Juice 3 tablespoons blackcurrants with the star fruit, guavas, apple, pineapple, and lime. Add 4 tablespoons plain yogurt to the blender with the rest of the ingredients.

guava, pineapple & kiwi fruit
Omit the star fruit and juice 1 peeled kiwi fruit with the guava, apple, pineapple, and lime.

guava, pineapple & star fruit with banana
Prepare the basic recipe, omitting the avocado. Substitute 1/2 ripe banana, and add 2 tablespoons plain yogurt to the blender with the rest of the ingredients.

index